love
welcome
serve

love welcome serve

Recipes that GATHER *and* GIVE

amy nelson hannon

CENTER
STREET®

NEW YORK   NASHVILLE

Center Street
Hachette Book Group
1290 Avenue of the Americas, New York, NY 10104
centerstreet.com
twitter.com/centerstreet

First Edition: November 2017

Center Street is a division of Hachette Book Group, Inc. The Center Street name and logo are trademarks of Hachette Book Group, Inc.

The publisher is not responsible for websites (or their content) that are not owned by the publisher.

The Hachette Speakers Bureau provides a wide range of authors for speaking events. To find out more, go to www.HachetteSpeakersBureau.com or call (866) 376-6591.

Scriptures taken from the Holy Bible, New International Version®, NIV®. Copyright © 1973, 1978, 1984, 2011 by Biblica, Inc.™ Used by permission of Zondervan. All rights reserved worldwide. www.zondervan.com The "NIV" and "New International Version" are trademarks registered in the United States Patent and Trademark Office by Biblica, Inc.™

Food photography by Amy Nelson Hannon. All photos of Amy by Meredith Brown.

Print book interior design by Timothy Shaner, nightanddaydesign.biz

Library of Congress Cataloging-in-Publication Data has been applied for.

ISBNs: 978-1-4789-9291-2 (paper over board), 978-1-4789-9289-9 (ebook)

Printed in the United States of America

WOR

10   9   8   7   6   5   4   3   2

This book is for Sam, Grace, Luke, and Isaac.
You will never, ever know the depth of joy in my heart
that comes from making a home for you.
You are the most precious objects
of my kitchen affections.

CONTENTS

MY HEART

I FEED PEOPLE.

My husband, my children, and anyone who walks in my door.

New faces on my street, and old friends.

People who have babies, job changes, and water damage.

People who are celebrating.

People who are grieving.

My town's high school football coaches.

The UPS man who knocks on the door.

Churchfolk, kinfolk, menfolk, womenfolk.

And just about any other folks who come across my path.

Why do I feed people? Because I believe with my whole heart that people who are cooked for feel cared for. I've believed that for as long as I can remember. This way of love was modeled by my grandmother Euna Mae Nelson, who fed her Circle group, her Sunday school class, and her grandchildren every Wednesday when we'd come over to play. She made compassion meals for people who were hurting. She donated treats to area bake sales. She hosted and fed her family's families on sled-worthy snow days, any given pretty afternoon, and every Easter and Christmas for as long I can remember.

Euna Mae had a round wooden stool with a cushioned top that she'd let me pull right up between her sink and her stove—which was exactly in the middle of "in the way." I'd ask questions, and she'd answer. I'd sit on my knees and watch her tend to her gooey, slow-stirred, homemade mac 'n' cheese with noodles that, at the time, seemed as big as my face. I learned over time how to recognize when the macaroni and cheese was ready to be taken out of the oven because the cheese and butter were all melted in and the edges had juuust started to dry out. Sometimes I'd stand right next to her while she made her famous peach fried pies that my daddy and his brothers would practically wrestle over. I'd watch her test the heat of her pan with the first pie, sometimes too hot and sometimes just right. (Too hot meant burning a pie, which made her madder than a wet hen!) I would stand nose-up to the kitchen counter, watching and waiting, while the still-sizzling pies drained right in front of me on brown paper bags from our small-town grocery store. At the time I didn't think a thing about parking myself right in the action zone of her small kitchen. But as I got older, with a kitchen of my own, and reflected back on those days in the kitchen with Euna Mae, I realized why she never shooed me away. She was *intentional kitchening*. She knew that making and serving food was a means to an end, and that the "end" was impacting the lives of people for the better. And in this case, that life was mine.

Because feeding people is the way love was shown to me and the way I show love, I've become aware in the last several years of how folks have gotten away from feeding their families, from opening their doors to friends and neighbors, and from using the ministry of food to love on people. Everyone's gotten busy, noses down in their phones and hustling all about. Everyone's gotten wrapped up in making things just so, like a Pinterest board or a staged social media photo. (Emphasis on the word *staged*.) The result is excuses, comparisons, closed doors, and missed opportunities to show people they're cared for. Isn't that a shame? Let me tell you, I became stirred on the inside about encouraging and equipping folks to embrace hospitality—intentional kitchening—so people wouldn't miss one more minute of the love that happens when they make and serve food to their people.

One day when my husband, Sam, was working from home, I went into his office and, with a lump in my throat, told him that I felt as if God was urging me to do something bigger. I didn't know what that "bigger something" was, and it scared the daylights out of me. I liked my life at home, doing for-hire projects here and there, keeping my house, nurturing my relationships, and ya know, hanging out. But I'm telling you, this urge was undeniably strong. I knew only two things: (1) I had a growing desire to inspire folks to use their homes and kitchens to get into the lives of people, and (2) my heart raced so hard I couldn't sleep because I sensed God had something in mind that He wanted me to do about it. So I prayed and waited. And I wish you could've been a mouse in my pocket for the next six months and witnessed all the things that came together to steer me toward my first "big" move.

With purpose and some divine prompting, I opened a kitchen boutique down the street from my house named after my grandmother Euna Mae, with hopes of encouraging and equipping folks to live out authentic hospitality, to inspire intentional kitchening. Y'all, I was forty-one years old and had never worked in retail. Gosh, for that matter, I had never even had five consecutive days with a shower and makeup. But it was clear as a bell that it was the step I was supposed to take, the purpose that had been stirred up in my heart that one teary-eyed day with Sam. I had peace and passion, and the people responded. And they're still responding.

They're responding to a lifestyle of hospitality found in 1 Peter 4:8–11. So what exactly do those verses say? "Above all, love each other deeply, because love covers over a multitude of sins. Offer hospitality to one another without grumbling. Each of you should use whatever gift you have received to serve others, as faithful stewards of God's grace in its various forms . . . so that in all things God may be praised through Jesus Christ. . . ."

Love deeply. Welcome gladly. Serve faithfully. So that in all things God may be praised. These three words captured my heart: Love. Welcome. Serve.

The "Love Welcome Serve" lifestyle means living with an awareness that people have emotional, spiritual, and physical needs, and using the comfort and ministry of food to respond to those needs, demonstrating the goodness of God in their lives. It's opening your heart to impact theirs. It's opening your home to give people a place to belong. Love Welcome Serve is deliberate and considerate. Simply said, it's intentional kitchening. Purposeful plating. Lovin' on people with lasagna. Can the people be strangers? Yes. Company? Yes. Your spouse and kids? Yes. Your mail carrier? Yes. Crown roast or boxed macaroni and cheese? Yes. Food is the means to an end, and the "end" is to impact the lives of people for the better. Love Welcome Serve.

I love the way Sally Clarkson says it in her book *The Lifegiving Home*: "There is something about preparing food and sharing it that enhances relationships, builds community, and even fosters spiritual connection." My goodness, she is so right! And you want to know what else? When you purposefully pour yourself into others, the treat will be yours, too! There's something unique and magical about serving. It'll come right back around and squeeze your heart.

MY HOPE

As with my retail store, my social media presence, my loud mouth, and about every other platform the good Lord's given to me, my hope for this book is that you will be encouraged and equipped to live out authentic, intentional, life-giving hospitality right there in your own kitchens and homes.

I hope to encourage you to . . .

- see that cooking for your family is an enormous privilege and can create treasured memories and lifelong warm fuzzies.
- look for folks who need to feel that they matter and invite them into your home to be seen and cared for.
- be the one who finally takes the step of inviting rather than waiting to be invited.
- tune your heart to hear others' needs and respond with a pot pie at their door.
- view your home as one of the warmest and most effective tools to love on your kids, their friends, your neighbors, the new family in town, and more.

- realize that hospitality is about others, not you, and enjoy the freedom and peace that it brings.
- pray that God will blow the doors of your home wide open so that out of your kitchen and around your table, lives will be changed for the better.

I hope to equip you with . . .

- family-friendly recipes that you can make on busy weeknights or on slow Sunday afternoons.
- dishes that you can fix for crowds that stretch and feed bellies and have reasonable shortcuts so that you're able to welcome them with a happy heart.
- make-ahead recipes that are perfect for weekend company, allowing you to spend your time visiting and enjoying their faces.
- portable comfort meals that can be easily prepared and transported, and that make good leftovers for the times when you feel prompted to serve someone who has a crisis—or just deserves a little care.
- suggestions for stocking your pantry and fridge so that you're prepared to pull off a quick, yummy meal for starving teenagers. (And they're always starving, y'all. Always.)
- helpful tips for making ahead, freezing, doubling, preparing, taking shortcuts, and more.
- food that just plain tastes good—crowd-pleasers and belly-fillers that anyone can make!

So, you've got this book in your hands, you've listened to me *rah-rah-ree* about living a life of authentic hospitality, and in the pages that follow, you'll be all set for gathering and giving, serving and sharing food! Good food, great impact, and big blessings are about to be yours! Now let's get in our kitchens and cook the fool out of some food, and change the world one pot pie at a time!

Intentional kitchening, y'all.

love welcome serve,

A FEW THINGS ABOUT A FEW THINGS

I love the part of a cookbook where the author shares all kinds of hints about ingredients and equipment to inspire and help readers on their journey through the book. So, here are a few of my own thoughts that I hope will help you with this book, with these recipes, and with the mission of intentional kitchening!

INGREDIENTS

For the longest time, I didn't believe that the quality of ingredients made much of a difference in my cooking. But y'all, it makes a *big* difference. So, here's my number one encouragement to help you make a big splash in your cooking: Buy the best ingredients you can afford. Good olive oil, good vanilla, good cheese, and so on. And buy natural ingredients whenever you can.

Use **real lemon juice** rather than that artificial stuff in the plastic bottle. I've considered flying an airplane pulling a banner that says, "Squeeze your own lemons!" But maybe this will do the trick.

If you choose not to make your own chicken stock (which is fine, but I urge you to try making it at least once—see my recipe on page 171), then buy good-quality **chicken stock** rather than chicken broth. Chicken stock is generally made with bones—and we all know that there's flavor in those bones! Chicken broth is usually made with only meat. Same goes for **beef stock** over beef broth; it's just so much richer.

Choose **full-fat ingredients**, not low-calorie or low-fat. I just believe it's the way God intended it. So eat cream cheese in moderation, but when you do, do it with gusto. Then go run your block or plank a little longer at your workout class.

Use real **mayonnaise**. The creamy salad dressing that sits beside mayonnaise at the grocery is not a substitute. My favorite mayonnaise is Hellmann's. Always and forever.

I believe so firmly in **shredding your own cheese**, y'all. It's my soapbox. It's more natural and so much creamier, especially when you're melting it into a soup, like my White Chicken Chili (page 89). The only cheese that I buy pre-shredded is mozzarella, for a recipe like Layered Spaghetti Pie (page 114), because mozzarella is so soft that it's nearly impossible to shred. But cheddar, Monterey Jack, Parmesan, and the like, I shred.

In this book, I call for **granulated garlic** rather than garlic powder. They are very similar in flavor, but granulated garlic has a little more texture. You can substitute garlic powder if you prefer, as they are virtually interchangeable. What is not interchangeable is garlic salt. As a matter of fact, there's no real need for you to buy garlic salt—just good granulated garlic (or garlic powder) and salt. That'll do.

When in doubt, use **unsalted butter**. It's not a crime to use salted butter, but with unsalted I know I can control the amount of salt in a recipe. I buy butter by the wheelbarrow. It can freeze for several months so I know I always have backup.

If I'm not making my own marinara, I look for a high-quality **store-bought tomato sauce**. Choose a brand that has the fewest number of ingredients on the label. And it never hurts to stir a tablespoon of butter into your jarred sauce when it's simmering on the stove to add a little richness and to round out the acidity.

Regular **all-purpose flour** is what fills my giant glass jar on the counter. I purchase special flour like cake flour or bread flour only when I need it for a particular recipe. And here's a tip: Before you reach in to scoop and measure out your flour, use a whisk to stir it up and loosen it a little. You'll get a more accurate measurement with light, loose flour.

Baking soda and baking powder can both expire, which means that they won't add the necessary rise and texture to your baked goods. To test baking soda, stir a teaspoon into a little cup of white vinegar. It will fizz and bubble if it's still fresh. To test baking powder, stir a teaspoon into boiling water and it should vigorously fizz, too. If they don't bubble up, then it's time to replace them!

For all my baking, I use **Baker's Joy baking spray** because it has flour in it. There's nothing more heartbreaking than turning out half of a Bundt cake with the other half stuck in the pan. A good coating of Baker's Joy will do the trick every time.

Vanilla extract is absolutely one of my favorite ingredients. I almost always give the bottle a long, slow whiff before I pour it into the mixer or bowl. Spend a little extra on good vanilla like Nielsen-Massey, or make your own with lots and lots of beans.

You're gonna have to search for it, but look high and low to find **ground Vietnamese cinnamon**. It is so much sweeter and more flavorful than regular cinnamon. I use cinnamon in so much of my baking, and even in a few dry rubs for meat. Vietnamese cinnamon will change everything about your cinnamon rolls, taking them from good to *Oh my word!*

A WELL-EQUIPPED KITCHEN

My kitchen equipment gets a serious workout, between cooking for my family and friends and testing and making recipes for my blog and cooking show. There are a few things I simply cannot live without. They are my high-performing workhorses. Some of these must-haves aren't pricey one bit, while others are more of an investment. I encourage you to invest in the good stuff if you can. Or put it on your Christmas wish list. But do get a few pieces of high-quality cookware and at least one premium knife in your life. You'll be so glad you did! Here are what I consider the essentials for a well-equipped kitchen:

- a good skillet with a nonstick coating
- a hard-working cast iron skillet
- a heavy-duty Dutch oven, like Le Creuset or Staub
- several restaurant-quality sheet pans in various sizes
- an Epicurean cutting board (It feels like wood but goes in the dishwasher!)
- a pretty wooden cutting board that doubles as a server
- functional prep bowls and pretty mixing bowls that can be used for prep and presentation
- a stand mixer like KitchenAid or Smeg
- a food processor
- wooden spoons and utensils
- serving platters
- oven-to-table ceramics
- several sets of measuring cups and spoons
- lots of flour sack towels
- four knives: paring, utility, chef's, serrated bread (My go-to knife is the 7-inch Zwilling J. A. Henckels Pro Rocking Santoku.)
- plenty of storage containers and mason jars with lids
- one quality, non-stick bundt pan like Nordic Ware
- plenty of take-out containers and aluminum foil pans to make sharing food a breeze

A WELL-STOCKED PANTRY

A well-stocked pantry is at the ready to make and share food! I do a lot of grocery shopping—sometimes I'm at the grocery twice a day, God's honest truth. On the one hand, there are ingredients that I buy specifically for recipes on my weekly menu or for recipes that I'm testing. But then there are the staples that I always have on hand. Always. These groceries, pantry items, and frozen goods can be easily tossed together to make a quick brunch, comforting pasta dish, hearty soup, or yummy salad. They've proven reliable and trustworthy when I've needed them, so they're always on my list and in my pantry!

PASTAS AND GRAINS
- dried pasta
- rice and quinoa

CANS AND BOXES
- canned tomatoes (whole, diced, crushed, paste)
- chicken stock and beef stock
- canned beans

- jarred tomato sauce/marinara
- canned diced green chiles
- jarred roasted red peppers
- nuts
- olives
- jarred marinated artichokes

BAKING INGREDIENTS

- all-purpose flour
- baking powder and baking soda (Yes, you need both!)
- chocolate chips
- sugars: white, brown, and powdered
- vanilla extract
- unsweetened cocoa powder
- boxed brownie and cake mixes for emergencies and quick-start desserts

CONDIMENTS AND SAUCES

- jams and jellies
- vinegars (Apple cider vinegar and champagne vinegar are my faves!)
- BBQ sauce
- honey
- several mustards: yellow, whole-grain, and Dijon
- olive oil
- canola oil or other neutral vegetable oil
- Worcestershire sauce

IN THE FRIDGE

- bacon
- cheeses (Parmesan, cheddar, mozzarella, and something strong like blue cheese or goat cheese, for crumbling)
- cream cheese
- eggs (I use large brown, cage-free eggs.)
- real mayonnaise
- whole milk
- whole sour cream
- unsalted butter
- heavy whipping cream
- refrigerated pie crust

FRESH PRODUCE

- cherry or grape tomatoes
- garlic
- lemons
- onions (yellow and red)
- potatoes
- apples (Granny Smith and Honeycrisp are my favorites for snacking and baking.)
- spinach and mixed greens for salads
- fresh herbs, like rosemary, basil, and cilantro

IN THE FREEZER

- ground beef (preferably 80 percent lean)
- boneless, skinless chicken breasts
- shrimp
- frozen fruits
- frozen vegetables
- frozen dinner rolls
- tortillas
- homemade dishes (Double a recipe when you're making it and freeze one for another day!)

SPICE CABINET

- crushed red pepper flakes
- Creole seasoning (such as Tony Chachere's)
- dried herbs (thyme, oregano, rosemary)
- spices (ground cumin, ground cinnamon, chili powder, granulated garlic, granulated onion, dry mustard)
- black pepper (both ground and cracked)
- table salt and sea salt

No. 1

BITES THAT WELCOME

*To invite someone into your home is to take charge of their
happiness for as long as they are under your roof.*
—J. Brillat-Savarin, *The Physiology of Taste*

AUNT LORI'S CHEESE BALL

My husband is the middle of three boys. His big brother and his little brother both married girls who can cook. So when I say that Hannon holidays are done right, I mean they're done right. My sister-in-law Lori has made this cheese ball for every gathering and holiday since she's been in the family. The adults love it, and the kids do, too. Around my house before we gather with the Hannons, my kids start asking, "Is Aunt Lori bringing her cheese ball?" Yes, my dear children. Yes, she is. Quite frankly, I think Aunt Lori suspects that if she didn't show up with this cheese ball in hand, we'd turn her away at the door. Blood is *not* thicker than cheese ball. Not in our family, anyway.

---

3 (8-ounce) packages cream
  cheese, at room temperature
1 tablespoon Accent seasoning
1 tablespoon Worcestershire sauce
6 green onions, chopped
1 (3-ounce) jar real bacon bits
1½ cups pecan chips
Crackers, for serving

In a medium bowl, combine the very soft cream cheese, Accent, Worcestershire, chopped green onions, and real bacon bits. Using a rubber spatula, spread, mash, and stir to combine well. Put the pecan chips in a shallow bowl.

Lay out two pieces of plastic wrap on the counter so it's at the ready when your hands are a mess! Divide the cream cheese mixture in half and form into two balls. Roll each ball in the pecan chips, gently pressing them into the cream cheese. Lay each cheese ball in the middle of a piece of plastic wrap. Wash your hands, then wrap up the cheese balls and refrigerate for an hour or more. Allow to sit at room temperature for at least 15 minutes before serving with good crackers.

LITTLE TOASTS

We absolutely love these crunchy Italian crostini. Little toasts are so handy when you have folks over, as we so often do. They're simple to make, they're delicious, they store for a week, and they can be served so many ways! Serve them with baked dips. Top them with Roasted Red Pepper–Pimento Cheese (page 21). Pile them on a meat and cheese board. Or drop them into a good soup. Savory, crunchy delights!

1 (10-ounce) baguette
Olive oil
½ teaspoon salt
½ teaspoon ground black pepper
½ teaspoon granulated garlic
½ teaspoon paprika
½ teaspoon dried oregano

Set the oven to 375°F.

Using a bread knife, cut the baguette into ¼-inch slices. Brush both sides of the slices with olive oil and lay them out in a single layer on a sheet pan. In a small bowl, mix the salt, pepper, garlic, and paprika. Rub the dried oregano between your fingers as you add it to the seasoning blend. Stir to combine. Sprinkle the tops of the oiled baguette slices with the seasoning blend.

Bake for 12 minutes, then turn over the slices and bake for another 10 to 12 minutes, or until they're crisp and golden. Remove from the oven and allow to cool completely. Store in an airtight container for up to a week.

CREAMY CHIPPED BEEF DIP

This recipe for creamy chipped beef dip is a hybrid of Aunt Lori's Cheese Ball (page 2) and my friend Corrie's dip that she brought to a dinner party when we were in our twenties. Good heavens— it's creamy, savory, salty, nutty, and has a little tang from the sour cream. You can stir it up in advance, spread it into a pretty pie plate, and bake it just before serving time. I usually serve it with crispy crackers, though it's equally delicious with hunks of toasted sourdough bread.

1 (8-ounce) package cream cheese, at room temperature
½ cup whole sour cream
2 cups shredded cheddar cheese
1 teaspoon Worcestershire sauce
1 (2½-ounce) jar dried beef, chopped
2 or 3 green onions, chopped
½ to 1 cup chopped pecans

Set the oven to 325°F. Lightly grease a 9-inch pie plate or an 8-inch square baking dish.

In a bowl, mix the cream cheese, sour cream, cheddar, Worcestershire, dried beef, and chopped green onions until everything is well combined. Spoon the mixture into the prepared baking dish and scatter the chopped pecans over the top. Bake for 35 minutes, or until the dip is melty and the pecans look toasty and delicious.

Note

Instead of a pie plate or baking dish, you can spoon the mixture into a hollowed-out sourdough round and place it on a sheet pan. The baking time will be about the same.

TEXAS FIRECRACKERS

I'm an Arkansas girl, but my best college friend is from Texas and she introduced these crackers to me, thus the name. And y'all, they are so good! It will go against everything you believe in to drown these crackers in savory, delicious oil. But something magical and scientific happens, and the crackers soak up the oil and coat themselves in seasoned, herby goodness while holding their crisp! We have these on the counter for most life events and gatherings. We serve them with chili, soups, and hot sandwiches, or even with just a smear of peanut butter right on them.

4 sleeves saltine crackers

1 cup canola oil

1 (1-ounce) packet ranch dressing mix

1 to 2 tablespoons red pepper flakes

1 tablespoon dried dill

1 teaspoon granulated garlic

Unwrap the four sleeves of saltine crackers and stand them on their sides like dominoes in a large plastic container with a tight-fitting lid. In a glass measuring cup, whisk together the canola oil, ranch dressing mix, red pepper flakes, dried dill, and granulated garlic. Pour the seasoned oil over all the crackers, up and down the rows. Let stand for about 5 minutes, cover the container, and flip it upside down so that all the oily, herby goodness that fell to the bottom is now on the top and can soak the crackers from the other end! Flip the container every 30 minutes or so, eventually giving them a gentle shake all around. The crackers will be ready to eat in about 2 hours.

SISTER'S FAVORITE SPINACH DIP

I have one daughter. As in many homes across the South, we call her "Sister," or "Sis" for short. That girl of mine loves spinach more than just about anything. This baked spinach dip is Sister's favorite. I make it for her birthdays and when she's home for the weekend. It stands out from other spinach dips that you may know because, among all the creaminess, it has a little heat from jalapeños and spicy chile tomatoes, and it's sweet from sautéed onions. Spoon any leftovers (if you have them) on a baked potato or grill it between two pieces of bread. Sister knows, y'all. Sister knows.

1 tablespoon unsalted butter

2 small sweet onions, finely chopped

1 (10-ounce) package frozen spinach, thawed

1½ cups shredded mild cheddar cheese

1½ cups shredded Monterey Jack cheese

1 (8-ounce) package cream cheese, at room temperature

2 tablespoons jarred chopped jalapeños

1 (10-ounce) can diced tomatoes with green chiles

½ cup half-and-half

1 teaspoon granulated garlic

Tortilla chips, Little Toasts (page 5), or fancy crackers, for serving

Set the oven to 350°F. Lightly grease a 9-inch pie plate or 8-inch baking dish.

In a skillet, melt the butter over medium heat and sauté the onions until tender and golden. Remove from the heat.

Working with a handful at a time, squeeze the spinach nearly dry and transfer to a bowl. Add the shredded cheeses, cream cheese, sautéed onions, and jalapeños. Drain the can of tomatoes almost entirely, leaving a little bit of liquid, and add to the bowl. Add the half-and-half. Stir everything together well, then season with the granulated garlic and stir again.

Spread the dip into the greased pie plate or baking dish and bake for 20 minutes or so, until it's melted and bubbly and browning a bit on the top. Serve with your choice of dippers.

PEPPADEW AND PESTO CROSTINI

Sam and I discovered an appetizer in Dallas years ago, and it's the stuff that dreams are made of: peppadew peppers with their sweet heat, basil pesto that is herby and nutty, goat cheese with its undeniable tang, and sweet honey. As with many of my recipes, I taste and dissect every bite of our restaurant favorites so I can get home and make them myself. Although the appetizer we ate in Dallas was prepared in an entirely different manner, this crostini recipe is the way I've taken those flavors that we're wild about and made a version of my own. They. Are. Fabulous!

1 (10-ounce) baguette

Olive oil

16 ounces fresh mozzarella

1½ cups finely chopped peppadew peppers

3 tablespoons pesto

Honey

2 ounces crumbled goat cheese

Cracked black pepper

Set the oven to 375°F.

Using a good bread knife, cut the baguette into ½-inch slices. Brush both sides of the slices with olive oil and lay them out in a single layer on a sheet pan. Bake for 15 minutes, turn them over, and bake for another 5 to 7 minutes, or until crisp and golden. Set aside.

Cut the fresh mozzarella into 18 slices and lay them out on a paper towel–lined tray. Place another paper towel on top of the slices and gently press to absorb extra moisture. Cut the slices of mozzarella in half and place a piece on each crostini on the sheet pan. In a small bowl, stir together the finely chopped peppadew peppers and pesto. Scoop about a teaspoon of the peppadew mixture on top of the mozzarella on the crostini.

Move the top oven rack to the highest position and preheat the broiler for 3 minutes on low. Place the sheet pan of crostini on the rack and broil with the oven door slightly cracked for 3 to 4 minutes, watching very closely. The toasts will start to get good and dark brown on the edges, the mozzarella will melt, and the peppers will sizzle and roast. Remove the sheet pan from the oven. Drizzle the entire pan with honey. Top the crostini with crumbled goat cheese and cracked black pepper. Serve warm.

Note

Peppadew peppers are sweet piquanté peppers. They are often found in the fresh olive bar at your gourmet grocer. And if you're lucky, you may find them jarred in the aisles. It's worth the search to find them because their flavor is to die for! But if you can't locate them, you can substitute roasted red peppers instead.

TOASTED COCONUT AND BACON POPCORN

This popcorn is so good that everyone I've ever made it for has swooned themselves into a frenzy. This fabulous flavor combination was inspired by a trip to the Donut Hole while we were vacationing along the beaches of 30A. I was just about to throw away the empty box, but there were some good crumbles left in the bottom from my coconut doughnut and Sam's maple-bacon doughnut. And y'all, that pinch of coconut, bacon, and sweet glaze was out of this world. I decided then and there that I was going to recreate that flavor in some amazing treat. This is that treat!

8 cups freshly popped unsalted popcorn

2 cups sweetened shredded coconut

12 slices bacon, cut into ½-inch pieces

6 (2-ounce) squares white chocolate almond bark

Cayenne pepper

Spread out the popcorn on a large sheet pan to cool, and pick out any unpopped kernels.

Meanwhile, in a large skillet, sauté the shredded coconut over medium heat until parts of it are toasted and browned. Transfer to a plate to cool.

Wipe out the skillet and return it to the stove. Add the bacon and sauté over medium heat until crisp and brown. Transfer to a paper towel–lined tray and allow to cool. Chop the bacon into small, crumbly bits.

In a microwave-safe bowl, melt the almond bark in 1-minute intervals until smooth. Pour the popcorn into your biggest bowl, then pour the melted almond bark over the popcorn. Gently fold and stir until coated. Stir in the toasted coconut and toss to coat. Then stir in the bacon bits and toss to coat. Spread out the popcorn on a large sheet pan lined with parchment. Sprinkle a pinch or two of cayenne pepper over the whole pan. Allow the popcorn to cool, then break it into clumps. Transfer the popcorn to a large bowl and watch your guests swoon. This is best if eaten when freshly made, which won't be a problem.

Note

I like to make popcorn in my big stockpot over medium heat: ½ cup of kernels to 3 tablespoons of canola oil.

MAMA'S LEMON PEPPER CREAM CHEESE

It's no secret that we love our cream cheese in the South. And my mother is no exception. She made this lemon pepper cream cheese for Sunday school gatherings, for her bridge group, and for our family nearly every time our beloved Razorbacks played on TV. It's about as easy as it comes, but it's *big* on flavor—peppery, tart, and creamy! To this day, Mama serves it in an antique leaded-glass dish with a pretty spreader and butter crackers. And we eat it until the roofs of our mouths have had enough.

⅓ cup lemon pepper seasoning
Grated zest of 1 lemon
1 (8-ounce) package cream cheese
Crackers, for serving

In a wide, shallow bowl, stir together the lemon pepper seasoning and lemon zest. Lay the block of cream cheese in the bowl and gently press it into the seasoning. Turn the cream cheese, covering all sides in the seasoning. Carefully lift the cream cheese out and place it on a pretty plate or butter dish. Cover with plastic wrap and refrigerate for at least 4 hours or overnight. The longer the cream cheese sits in the lemon pepper seasoning, the better it will be! About 30 minutes before serving, remove the cream cheese from the refrigerator and allow it to sit at room temperature so it'll spread easily onto your favorite crackers.

Makes about 64

EVERYTHING PIGS IN A BLANKET WITH BROWN SUGAR–HONEY MUSTARD

Pigs in a blanket with yellow mustard are a childhood favorite. Okay, they're an adult favorite, too, if we're being entirely honest with each other. Even Ina Garten has been known to claim that she loves to serve them at get-togethers! Well, these Everything Pigs in a Blankets are the grown-up version of that childhood favorite. They are perfect for watch parties. Each pig is smothered in melted butter seasoned with an "everything bagel" mix of poppy seeds, dried onions, garlic, and more. The brown sugar–honey mustard is sweet, tangy, and sooo good.

16 tablespoons (2 sticks) unsalted butter
1 tablespoon poppy seeds
1 tablespoon dried minced onion
1 teaspoon granulated garlic
½ teaspoon dry mustard
Red pepper flakes
2 (8-ounce) tubes refrigerated crescent dough sheets (not triangles)
2 (12-ounce) packages cocktail smokies

For the sauce
½ cup Dijon-style mustard
1 teaspoon stone-ground mustard
5 tablespoons brown sugar
3 teaspoons honey
⅛ teaspoon cayenne pepper

Set the oven to 375°F.

In a small saucepan, melt the butter over low heat. Stir in the poppy seeds, dried minced onion, granulated garlic, dry mustard, and several shakes of red pepper flakes. Remove the pan from the heat and set aside.

Place a sheet of parchment paper on your work surface and roll out one crescent dough sheet. Cut the sheet in half down the center, then cut those two pieces in half the other way. Continue making vertical and horizontal cuts until you have 32 small strips (about 1½ inches long).

Drain and pat dry one package of cocktail smokies and wrap each smokie in a piece of dough. Line them up on a sheet pan, seam-side down.

Repeat with the remaining dough sheet and smokies on another sheet pan.

Whisk the seasoned butter mixture, stirring up the goodness that has settled to the bottom. Spoon a little over each wrapped smokie, making sure to dig down deep into the butter mixture so all the smokies have a little onion, garlic, and poppy seed on top! The butter will pour down the sides and pool below the smokies, which creates buttery magic when they're finished baking. Bake for 14 to 15 minutes, or until they're golden. Allow to cool for several minutes before transferring to a serving platter.

Meanwhile, whisk together the mustards, brown sugar, honey, and cayenne in a bowl. Stir until the sugar dissolves. Taste and adjust the seasonings. Serve with the warm pigs in a blanket.

FRIED GREEN TOMATOES
WITH ZESTY CREAM SAUCE

I ate my first fried green tomato in Savannah, Georgia, when I was in my thirties. And y'all, I wondered why on Earth they hadn't been a part of my life all along! Well, now that I've created this recipe, I've started putting fried green tomatoes on burgers and BLTs and serving them as late-summer bites for my people. They are crunchy and seasoned on the outside but so tangy and fresh on the inside. A dollop of lemony dill cream puts them right up there in the heavenlies. Read the recipe through and get your stations in order so you can work through these with ease! Please eat one when it's fresh off the skillet, and think of me.

FOR THE SAUCE

1 cup mayonnaise
1 tablespoon grated lemon zest
1 tablespoon minced fresh chives
½ teaspoon chopped fresh dill
Cayenne pepper

FOR THE TOMATOES

2 large eggs
1 cup seasoned croutons
1 cup panko bread crumbs
1 tablespoon Creole seasoning
3 large green tomatoes, cut into
  ½-inch-thick slices
Canola oil, for frying
Salt

Note

Green tomatoes are available only in the summer, from June-ish to September-ish. But you can substitute tomatillos, which have a longer season.

Set the oven to 200°F. Line one sheet pan with paper towels. Place a wire rack on a second sheet pan.

In a small bowl, whisk together the mayonnaise, lemon zest, chives, dill, and a pinch of cayenne. Taste and adjust the seasonings. Cover and chill the sauce while you prep and fry the tomatoes.

In a shallow dish or pie plate, lightly beat the eggs.

Put the croutons in a zip-top bag, press out the air and seal it, and pound the croutons into crumbs using a rolling pin or heavy kitchen utensil. Transfer the crumbs to another shallow dish or pie plate and add the panko and Creole seasoning. Mix well.

Lay out the green tomato slices in a single layer on the sheet pan lined with paper towels. Carefully press the tops of the tomatoes with another paper towel to absorb any extra moisture.

Working in batches of two or three tomato slices at a time, coat both sides of each slice in beaten egg, then carefully press both sides into the breading mixture. Pour enough canola oil into a large skillet to cover the bottom and heat the oil over medium heat. When the oil is hot, fry the battered tomatoes for about a minute or so on each side, or until crisp and golden. Transfer the fried tomatoes to the sheet pan lined with the wire rack. Salt them immediately, right out of the skillet. Keep the fried green tomatoes warm in the oven while you batter and fry the remaining slices.

Serve the fried green tomatoes warm with the chilled dipping sauce.

ROASTED RED PEPPER-PIMENTO CHEESE

I grew up on pimento cheese—not the homemade kind, but the store-bought kind. And it was still a delicious treat, if you ask me. We'd spread it on soft white bread, which is the way all good people of the South do it, and occasionally on crackers. My grandmother Euna Mae even baked hers in a little oven-safe dish like a hot cheesy dip! This recipe gets added flavor from roasted red peppers and a little extra kick from cayenne. It's also awful good with a dash or two of hot sauce if that's your thing!

- 4 ounces (half of an 8-ounce package) cream cheese, at room temperature
- 1 cup shredded sharp cheddar cheese
- 1 cup shredded Monterey Jack cheese
- ½ cup mayonnaise
- 2 tablespoons chopped jarred pimentos
- 2 tablespoons chopped jarred roasted red peppers
- ¼ teaspoon cayenne pepper
- ⅛ teaspoon granulated garlic
- Milk or half-and-half, as needed
- Salt
- Ground black pepper

In the bowl of a stand mixer fitted with the paddle attachment, cream the cream cheese, shredded cheeses, and mayonnaise until creamy. Mix in the chopped pimentos and roasted red peppers. Stir in the cayenne and granulated garlic. Stir in a teaspoon of milk (or half-and-half) at a time until it's the consistency you like. Add salt and black pepper to taste.

Serve right away, or cover and refrigerate until time to serve. Allow to sit at room temperature for at least 15 minutes before serving or spreading.

CREAM CHEESE SAUSAGE BALLS
AND JEZEBEL SAUCE

I've never met a person in my life who doesn't love sausage balls. They are such an easy starter to put out for your people to snack on. We also love them for breakfast. (If I'm being honest, we could indulge in them any time of day.) These sausage balls are dolled up with cream cheese and green onions, and then we dip them in a sweet-hot sauce that gets its name from a racy little gal in the Bible. And rightfully so, because these are spicy and shamefully good! Make them ahead and freeze for on-the-spot baking when you need something quick.

FOR THE SAUSAGE BALLS
- 1 pound hot ground breakfast sausage
- 1 (8-ounce) package cream cheese, at room temperature
- 1 cup shredded sharp cheddar cheese
- ¼ cup chopped green onions
- 1 cup baking mix (such as Bisquick)
- Cracked black pepper

FOR THE JEZEBEL SAUCE
- 1 cup peach preserves
- ½ cup pineapple preserves
- 1 teaspoon horseradish
- 1 teaspoon Worcestershire sauce
- 1 teaspoon apple cider vinegar
- 1 teaspoon red pepper flakes

Set the oven to 350°F. Line a sheet pan with parchment paper.

In a large mixing bowl, use a heavy wooden spoon to combine the ground sausage, cream cheese, cheddar, and green onions. Fold, stir, and chop at it with your spoon until it's as mixed as it can be. Add the baking mix and stir until it's well combined. Again, fold, stir, and chop.

Using a heaping tablespoon or a cookie scoop, form 30 round sausage balls and line them up on the parchment-lined sheet pan. Hit the tops of them with a good dose of cracked black pepper. Bake for 20 to 25 minutes, or until browned and sizzling.

Meanwhile, in a small bowl, stir together all the Jezebel sauce ingredients. Serve the warm sausage balls with the sauce for dipping.

Note

The Jezebel sauce will keep in an airtight container in the refrigerator for about 2 weeks, and in fact it's best made ahead and given time to develop good flavor. It's also delicious with pork or with crackers and cream cheese!

SEAFOOD FONDUE

I recently served this seafood fondue to a crew of eight adults who were at my house. A few of them let me know right off the bat that they weren't fans of seafood of any kind. But they quickly changed their tune when everyone else in the room was going on and on about how rich, buttery, and fabulous it was. Needless to say, there wasn't a drop left in the pan! This seafood fondue is a one-pot welcoming bite that requires a little chopping, a little stirring, and a little baking—and that's it! Inspired by an appetizer that Sam and I shared on a weekend getaway, this seafood fondue will win people's hearts. Serve it right out of a cast iron skillet or spooned into individual baking dishes.

1 tablespoon olive oil

1 tablespoon + 1 tablespoon unsalted butter

1 yellow onion, chopped

1½ cups chopped button or baby portobello (cremini) mushrooms

2 garlic cloves, chopped

3 tablespoons all-purpose flour

1¼ cups heavy whipping cream

2 teaspoons Creole seasoning

1½ cups shredded Monterey Jack cheese

8 ounces small raw shrimp, peeled, deveined, and tails removed, roughly chopped

6 ounces lump crab

2 ounces (2 big handfuls) baby spinach leaves, roughly chopped

Little Toasts (page 5) or sourdough bread hunks, for serving

Set the oven to 375°F.

In a large oven-safe skillet, heat the oil with 1 tablespoon butter over medium heat. Add the onion and sauté until just tender. Stir in the mushrooms and sauté for a few minutes, until they are tender and turn a pretty brown. Stir in the garlic and sauté for about 1 minute, or until fragrant. Reduce the heat to medium-low heat and stir in the remaining 1 tablespoon butter. Shake the flour over the sautéed vegetables and stir to coat. Cook for 1 minute. Slowly pour in the whipping cream and stir in the Creole seasoning. Stir over low heat until the mixture just begins to thicken. Stir in the cheese. Remove the pan from the heat. Stir in the chopped shrimp and lump crab. Then carefully fold in the fresh spinach; the warmth of the sauce will wilt the spinach.

Bake for 25 to 30 minutes, or until bubbly and browning on top. Allow to sit for 10 minutes before serving.

Note

I'm aware that lump crab is a splurge. But I'm telling you before you even try it, imitation crab just doesn't work in this recipe. This fondue is something special when you use the best ingredients!

DILLED CUCUMBER DIP

This cool, refreshing dip is one of my mother's signature dishes. It always reminds me of summer, when we would eat it with salty ruffled potato chips beside grilled burgers or with BBQ. But with a strong nod to tzatziki, it can be fancied up a little when served with soft, warmed pita triangles, perfect as a light welcoming bite for folks to dip into. It's also good alongside grilled chicken or fish.

½ **cup plain Greek yogurt**
½ **cup whole sour cream**
¼ **cup chopped fresh dill**
1 small shallot, minced
1 teaspoon grated lemon zest
2 teaspoons salt
½ **teaspoon granulated garlic**
Ground black pepper
1 English cucumber, peeled and diced
Hot sauce

In a medium bowl, stir together the yogurt, sour cream, dill, shallot, lemon zest, salt, garlic, and a pinch of pepper. Stir in the cucumber. Add a dash or two of hot sauce. Taste for seasoning and adjust. Cover and refrigerate for at least 30 minutes. Stir before serving, and taste one more time and adjust.

MEXICAN LAYERED CORNBREAD DIP

I have quite a list of bites that welcome because we tend to have a revolving front door. And it seems like everyone who enters this house is always hungry, which thrills my soul. One of my favorite dips that has run the gamut of parties and get-togethers is seven-layer dip. You know the one; I could eat my weight in it. But I've since taken that old stand-by and mashed it up with an old-fashioned Southern cornbread salad to come up with this amaaazing creation. Oh my word, the flavors! Fill up a big bowl with corn chip scoops, serve, and enjoy!

4 cups crumbled cornbread

1 (14-ounce) can black beans, rinsed and drained

1 (14-ounce) can pinto beans, rinsed and drained

1 pint cherry or grape tomatoes, quartered

2 tablespoons minced shallot

1 tablespoon minced garlic

2 to 3 tablespoons chopped fresh cilantro

1 teaspoon salt, plus a pinch

1 ripe avocado

2 cups whole sour cream

Juice of 2 limes

1 teaspoon ground cumin

½ teaspoon granulated garlic

½ cup milk

1 cup shredded Monterey jack cheese

1 cup shredded medium cheddar cheese

Chopped fresh chives, black olives, tomatoes, and/or jalapeños, for garnish

Spread out the crumbled cornbread in the bottom of a 9 x 13-inch casserole dish. Gently press down to even it out. Layer the black beans all over the cornbread, then scatter on the pinto beans to create a mixed bean layer.

In a small bowl, toss together the quartered cherry tomatoes, minced shallot, minced garlic, cilantro, and pinch of salt. Evenly distribute the tomato mixture on top of the beans.

Cut the avocado in half, remove the pit, and scoop the flesh into a medium bowl. Mash the avocado well, then add the sour cream, lime juice, cumin, granulated garlic, and 1 teaspoon salt. Stir well to combine. Add about half of the milk and stir, then add the remaining milk and stir until creamy. Carefully pour the avocado crema all around the pan, then gently spread it over the tomatoes without disturbing them. Top with the shredded cheeses. Cover and chill for at least 1 hour or overnight. Garnish with chopped chives, black olives, more tomatoes, or jalapeños, if desired.

Note

You can mix up a thicker version of the avocado crema by omitting the milk, then dollop it on pulled pork tacos, quesadillas, nachos, or enchiladas. We love it!

LOADED SOUTHERN GUACAMOLE

All I know is that I could live on guacamole for the rest of my life. We serve it as an afternoon snack, with enchiladas or pork tacos, and for many late-night powwows around the kitchen island. This recipe is a chunky loaded version with lots of stir-ins like bacon, goat cheese, and pimentos. It's one of our favorites.

4 slices bacon, chopped

4 ripe avocados

2 tablespoons minced shallot

1 tablespoon minced garlic

Juice of 2 limes

1 cup quartered cherry or grape tomatoes

1 (2-ounce) jar pimentos, drained

1 teaspoon salt

½ teaspoon ground cumin

Hot sauce

3 ounces crumbled goat cheese

1 tablespoon finely chopped fresh cilantro

Warmed tortilla chips, for serving

In a skillet, sauté the bacon over medium heat until crisp; transfer to a paper towel–lined plate. Set aside.

Halve and pit the avocados and scoop the flesh into a medium bowl. Right there in the bowl, use a knife to cut up the avocados into small bites. Add the shallot, garlic, and lime juice. Mash and stir the mixture together, leaving some chunks of avocado not mashed into a paste. Stir in the cherry tomatoes and pimentos. Stir in the salt and cumin, plus several dashes of hot sauce. Gently fold in about half of the crumbled goat cheese.

The best guacamole is probably tasted and adjusted three or four times until it's just right! Add more hot sauce, salt, or lime juice until it's to your liking. Use your fingers to crumble the crispy, cooled bacon into small bits; sprinkle them over the guacamole. Garnish with fresh cilantro and the remaining crumbled goat cheese. Serve with warmed tortilla chips and a bottle of hot sauce at the ready.

No. 2
Pickled, Tossed, and Chilled

❧❧❧

Spread love wherever you go.
Let no one ever come to you without leaving happier.
—Mother Teresa

EASY REFRIGERATOR PICKLES

There are sure signs of the seasons in every kitchen, like the scent of cinnamon and baked goods in fall, or savory, earthy soups when it's winter. Well, these refrigerator pickles mean it's summertime in our kitchen. I jar several batches of them every week and line them up on the top shelf of the refrigerator so the light shines on them when the door is opened. Just seeing them there thrills my soul. Sweet, tangy, vinegary, and fresh—we fork them on the sides of our plates all summer long and eat them straight out of the jars because we can't help it. I also love bringing a jar of these pickles with me to cookouts as a little something for the host!

1 or 2 seedless English cucumbers, thinly sliced

1 red onion, quartered and thinly sliced

Garlic cloves, peeled

White vinegar or other vinegar of your choice

Salt

Whole black peppercorns

Sugar

Fresh dill sprigs

For this recipe, you'll need a variety of glass jars with tight-fitting lids. In each jar, layer sliced cucumbers and onions, adding two garlic cloves per jar. Fill each jar halfway with vinegar, then finish off the jar with water. Add a teaspoon of salt, a teaspoon of black peppercorns, 2 or 3 tablespoons of sugar, and a sprig of fresh dill to each jar. Secure the lids and shake the pickles gently but well enough to dissolve the sugar and salt. Remove the lid and taste for seasonings; adjust as needed. Refrigerate for at least 2 hours before serving. Store in the refrigerator for about a week.

NANA'S CAULIFLOWER-OLIVE SALAD

My mom has made this fresh side dish for as long as I can remember. It's the most interesting combination of veggies, and we love it. Of course, in the South, you can toss just about anything in mayonnaise and we'd consider it a delicacy! It's important to start with whole olives and halve them lengthwise; don't fall into the convenience trap of buying sliced olives. The halved ones serve as little canoes that hold all the goodness. This salad is best if made a day before and chilled overnight to let the flavors develop.

¾ to 1 cup mayonnaise

½ teaspoon chopped fresh dill

½ teaspoon granulated garlic

¼ teaspoon dry mustard

½ head cauliflower, cut into bite-size florets

2 (6-ounce) cans medium pitted olives, drained, halved lengthwise

Salt

Ground black pepper

In a small bowl, stir together the mayonnaise (start with ¾ cup adding more as desired to make it creamier), fresh dill, granulated garlic, and dry mustard. In a medium bowl with a tight-fitting lid, toss together the cauliflower florets and halved black olives. Stir in the mayonnaise mixture. Place the lid on top and give the bowl a good shake the way Nana does! Taste and adjust the salt and pepper as needed. Chill for at least an hour, or preferably overnight, before serving.

Note

Nana always used Beau Monde seasoning when she made this salad. I've had trouble finding it in my grocery store, but it might be worth tracking down online. A little goes a long way, and it's awful good!

POTLUCK BROCCOLI SALAD

Nearly every Southern cook I know has a recipe for broccoli salad—I bet there are 573 variations of this dish. Some add bacon and different nuts, and I've even seen cheese. But this is the only way I've ever made it, and it's perfectly simple and delicious. So if you're early on in your cooking or you're well seasoned but late to the broccoli salad party, dog-ear this recipe. By all means take it to your potluck, and fix it for your people. It may be the best thing that has ever happened to you . . . and to broccoli.

1 cup golden raisins

1 cup mayonnaise

½ cup sugar

¼ cup white vinegar

1 head broccoli, cut into bite-size florets

½ red onion, finely chopped

1 cup cashews

Put the raisins in a small bowl and splash them with a few tablespoons of water. Heat them in the microwave for about 15 seconds, stir them, and let them soak in the water so they'll plump up and become tender.

Meanwhile, in a small bowl, whisk together the mayonnaise, sugar, and vinegar. In a medium bowl, toss together the broccoli, red onion, and cashews. Drain the raisins and add them to the mix. Stir in the mayonnaise sauce and coat everything well. Cover and chill for 30 minutes before serving.

ANYTIME SLAW

In my years, I've learned that creamy, tangy slaw is always a good idea. It makes a refreshing salad at a picnic or cookout, served on or alongside pulled pork, sloppy Joes, casual sandwiches, shrimp tacos, and more! It has saved my neck several times when I needed an inexpensive, quick something to help stretch a BBQ meal for a crowd. (Slaw saved the day in the summer of 2016, when we fed 60 college students who were serving as summer camp counselors!) It's truly perfect any time!

½ **head red cabbage**
½ **head green cabbage**
1 **seedless English cucumber, peeled and cut into matchsticks**
1½ **cups mayonnaise**
½ **cup apple cider vinegar**
¼ **cup honey**
Juice of 1 lime
1 **teaspoon sugar**
½ **teaspoon salt**

Using a mandoline, food processor, or your best knife skills, shred the cabbages. Toss the cabbage and cucumber in a large bowl. In a small bowl, whisk together the mayonnaise, vinegar, honey, lime juice, sugar, and salt. Taste and adjust the seasonings as needed. Pour over the cabbage mixture and toss well. Serve immediately, or cover and chill for up to 30 minutes before serving.

MAMA'S CRANBERRY SALAD

When Moses was leading the people through the Red Sea headed for the Promised Land, I feel sure that the women were carrying Jell-O salad. Okay, maybe not really. But Jell-O salad has been around for a long time—and for good reason. It can be made ahead, and everyone loves it, so it's perfect for BBQs, holidays, potlucks, picnics, and crossing the Red Sea with 3 million of your closest friends. This is my version of my mama's recipe.

2 cups hot water

2 (3-ounce) packages cranberry Jell-O (not sugar-free)

1 (14-ounce) can whole cranberry sauce

1 (20-ounce) can crushed pineapple

1 (15-ounce) can mandarin oranges, drained

1 (8-ounce) package cream cheese, at room temperature

1 cup whole sour cream

½ cup powdered sugar

1 teaspoon vanilla extract

In a large bowl, stir together the hot water and Jell-O packets until dissolved. While the liquid is still hot, stir in the whole cranberry sauce until it has dissolved and mixed in well. Stir in the crushed pineapple with its juice and the mandarin oranges. Pour the mixture into a 9 x 13-inch casserole dish and refrigerate for several hours, until set.

In the bowl of a stand mixer fitted with the paddle attachment, beat the cream cheese, sour cream, powdered sugar, and vanilla until smooth. Gently spread the topping over the set Jell-O. Serve immediately, or cover and refrigerate until serving time.

Note

Some folks can't imagine Jell-O salad without pecan chips. So if you're inclined, scatter them on top!

SHAVED BRUSSELS SALAD
WITH BEETS AND BACON

Brussels sprouts and beets have gotten a bad rap if you ask me. Bless their hearts, they just haven't been prepared well or served with the right things. My family is wild about both! This recipe is my own version of a salad we all ordered at a local restaurant one Sunday after church. There's so much to love! It's fresh, citrusy, earthy, creamy, and sweet. Plus there's bacon, which makes all things right in the world—even Brussels and beets.

---

20 Brussels sprouts

2 cups fresh arugula

2 cups baby spinach leaves

8 slices bacon, chopped

1 cup pine nuts

1 (16-ounce) jar whole baby pickled beets

1 (14-ounce) can mandarin oranges, drained

2 ounces goat cheese, crumbled

FOR THE DRESSING

¼ cup apple cider vinegar

2 tablespoons honey

1 tablespoon Dijon mustard

2 tablespoons chopped fresh chives

¾ cup olive oil

Salt

Ground black pepper

Trim the Brussels sprouts and use a sharp knife or a food processor to shave them into thin slices. In a large salad bowl, toss together the shaved Brussels, arugula, and spinach. Set aside.

In a saucepan, sauté the chopped bacon over medium heat until crisp. Transfer to a paper towel–lined plate. Pour off the bacon fat in the pan, wipe out the pan, and add the pine nuts. Toast the pine nuts over medium-low heat until fragrant and warm, stirring and tossing to be sure they don't burn. Transfer the pine nuts to the plate with the bacon.

Drain the pickled beets, lay them out on a paper towel–lined plate, and carefully pat the excess liquid off them with another paper towel. Add the beets to the shaved Brussels and greens, along with the mandarins, crisped bacon, toasted pine nuts, and crumbled goat cheese.

In a small bowl, whisk together the vinegar, honey, Dijon mustard, and chives. Drizzle in the olive oil, whisking continuously to combine. Add a pinch each of salt and pepper. Pour the dressing over the salad and toss well. This salad is best if served as soon as it's dressed.

Note

The salad and dressing can be prepared a few hours ahead and stored separately, covered, in the refrigerator. Toss the salad with the dressing just before serving.

PEAR AND GORGONZOLA SALAD
WITH APPLE-GINGER VINAIGRETTE

Serving fancy food isn't the norm around here. So when I hosted a five-course dinner party several years ago for a friend who was having a baby, I needed a pretty salad to serve following the soup course. This pear and Gorgonzola salad did the trick. It's light and sweet, with good texture and flavor. And it has since become a favorite that I make often! Serve this salad beside pretty pork, or pile it right on top of a grilled or baked salmon fillet for a quick, light meal.

8 slices bacon, chopped
¾ cup English walnut halves
10 cups arugula
1 pear, peeled, cored, and diced
3 ounces Gorgonzola cheese, crumbled

For the vinaigrette
¼ cup rice wine vinegar
3 tablespoons apple jelly, at room temperature
2 tablespoons honey
½ shallot, minced
½ teaspoon ground ginger
¾ cup olive oil
Salt
Ground black pepper

In a saucepan, sauté the chopped bacon over medium heat until crisp. Transfer to a paper towel–lined plate. Pour off the bacon fat from the pan, wipe out the pan, and add the walnut halves. Toast the walnut halves over medium-low heat until fragrant and warm, stirring and tossing to be sure they don't burn. Transfer the walnuts to the plate with the bacon.

In a large salad bowl, combine the arugula, pear cubes, crisped bacon, toasted walnut halves, and crumbled Gorgonzola.

In a small bowl, whisk together the vinegar, apple jelly, honey, shallot, and ginger. Drizzle in the olive oil, whisking continuously to combine. Add a pinch each of salt and pepper. Pour the dressing over the salad and toss to combine.

Note

For a little extra fancy, slice the pears, wrap them in bacon, and bake them in the oven until the bacon is crisp. It adds quite a punch of pizzazz to the plate!

If you're not a fan of Gorgonzola cheese, you can use goat cheese instead. In all honesty, goat cheese is my first love.

LEMON–POPPY SEED
FRIED CHICKEN SALAD

Chicken salad always sounds good to me, and this one is over-the-moon good. It's savory, crispy, sweet, tangy, creamy, and nutty all at once. The Greek yogurt and fresh lemon zest add a little tang, and then there's the fried chicken. You read that right: fried chicken, not tired old boiled chicken. Serve this chicken salad to your mama, your sister, your neighborhood ladies, your teacher, your preacher, and anyone else you love. Pile it on a buttery croissant, serve it with pretty crackers, or scoop it right into a Bibb lettuce boat on each plate.

1 cup plain Greek yogurt
¾ cup mayonnaise
2 tablespoons champagne vinegar
2 to 3 tablespoons honey
1 teaspoon Dijon mustard
1 teaspoon poppy seeds
Grated zest of 1 lemon
5 or 6 deli fried chicken tenders,
    cut into bite-size pieces
3 green onions (green parts only),
    chopped
2 or 3 celery stalks, chopped
1 cup sliced seedless red grapes
½ cup pecan halves
Salt
Ground black pepper

In a small bowl, whisk together the Greek yogurt, mayonnaise, champagne vinegar, honey, mustard, poppy seeds, and lemon zest. Taste and adjust, adding more honey, vinegar, or zest for your taste.

In a large bowl, combine the fried chicken bites, green onions, celery, grapes, and pecans. Stir in the mayonnaise mixture and toss to coat. Taste for salt and pepper. The quicker you serve it, the better, so the fried chicken crispies are still crispy.

CHOPPED BIBB SALAD
WITH EASY SUGARED PECANS

It's not every day that I rave about a salad, so you might want to perk up your ears for this one! This recipe is my version of a salad I eat every time I go to my favorite little pizza place. The best part about a chopped salad is that every bite has a yummy nugget of something—in this case, tender lettuce, smoky bacon, earthy hearts of palm, bright and juicy tomatoes, rich avocado, and sugared pecans. And then what happens to the creamy goat cheese when it meets the sweet honey vinaigrette is downright magical. It's a salad for the senses! Make it for your family or double it for guests. Add grilled chicken, salmon, or skirt steak to turn it into a main course!

FOR THE SUGARED PECANS
1½ tablespoons brown sugar
1½ teaspoons water
⅛ teaspoon vanilla extract
Salt
Ground cinnamon
1 cup pecan halves

FOR THE SALAD
8 slices thick-cut bacon, chopped
1 head Bibb lettuce (also known as butter lettuce)
1 cup grape or cherry tomatoes
1 (14-ounce) can hearts of palm
1 ripe avocado
¾ cup crumbled goat cheese

FOR THE VINAIGRETTE
¼ cup rice vinegar
2 tablespoon honey
Salt
Ground black pepper
¾ cup olive oil

Make the sugared pecans first, since they need to cool for at least an hour.

In a small bowl, stir together the brown sugar, water, vanilla, a tiny pinch of salt, and an even tinier pinch of cinnamon. The sugar and salt won't entirely dissolve, but that's okay.

In a saucepan, toast the pecans over medium heat for a few minutes, stirring often, until they smell nutty and aromatic. Stirring as you pour, drizzle the sugar mixture over the pecans and stir, stir, stir until they're coated. Remove them from the pan and spread them out on a parchment-lined sheet pan. Allow the sugared pecans to cool for at least an hour.

Next, make the salad. In a saucepan, sauté the chopped bacon over medium heat until nice and crispy. Transfer to a paper towel–lined plate. Set aside.

Now, have your favorite big salad bowl at the ready to throw in each of the ingredients as you chop them. Remove the leaves from the head of lettuce. Rinse and pat dry. Run your knife over the pieces for a big, rough chop, and transfer the pieces to the bowl. Rinse and halve the grape tomatoes lengthwise and add them to the bowl. Drain and slice the hearts of palm. Use your fingers to gently separate the rings and drop them into the bowl. Halve, pit, and dice the avocado and put it in the bowl. Top off the salad with the crispy bacon pieces, goat cheese, and sugared pecans.

Whisk together the vinegar, honey, and a pinch each of salt and pepper. Whisk in the olive oil. Drizzle over the salad and toss well.

PICKLED CHOW-CHOW

Chow-chow is a given around here. This sweet, vinegary, briny blend of bell peppers, cabbage, and carrots is prominently displayed at the grocery, and you can find it on the tailgates of trucks at the farmers' market. It's served as a starter, a side, and a garnish at many restaurants. It's for sale in my own store as well as taking up residence on the second shelf down in my refrigerator. We serve it over pintos, red beans and rice, pulled pork, eggs, and just about anything else we can think of.

1 cup apple cider vinegar

¼ cup water

¾ cup sugar

1 tablespoon kosher salt

1½ teaspoons mustard seeds

1 teaspoon red pepper flakes

1 teaspoon dry mustard

½ teaspoon ground ginger

1 yellow bell pepper, seeded and diced

1 orange bell pepper, seeded and diced

1 medium Vidalia onion, diced

1 cup carrot matchsticks

4 cups shredded green cabbage

In a large saucepan, combine the vinegar, water, sugar, salt, mustard seeds, red pepper flakes, dry mustard, and ginger. Bring just to a boil over medium-low heat, stirring to dissolve the sugar. Add the vegetables and stir to coat. Simmer over low heat for 20 to 30 minutes, stirring occasionally, until the vegetables are tender and have reduced. Remove from the heat and allow to cool to room temperature before transferring to glass jars with lids. Refrigerate overnight to allow the flavors to develop. Store in the refrigerator for up to 2 weeks.

CAESAR-Y KALE SALAD
WITH HOMEMADE CROUTONS

Right from the get-go, let me clarify why I'm calling this salad Caesar-y rather than flat-out Caesar. You see, I'm the girl who loves a Caesar salad, but in the back of my mind I'm always fearing the thought of raw eggs and anchovies. So I set out to develop a recipe that would be like a non-exotic cousin to Caesar. The result: all the creaminess, zinginess, and nuttiness that we love about Caesar, tossed with earthy kale and topped with magnificent Parmesan shavings. And then homemade croutons that will delight your soul!

½ cup mayonnaise

½ cup plain Greek yogurt

Juice of 2 lemons

1 teaspoon Dijon mustard

1 teaspoon Worcestershire sauce

1 cup grated Parmesan cheese, plus additional Parmesan shavings for serving

2 garlic cloves, minced

Salt

Ground black pepper

2 cups (1-inch) chunks sourdough bread

1 teaspoon dried oregano

Olive oil

1 bunch kale

Cracked black pepper

In a small bowl, whisk together the mayonnaise, yogurt, lemon juice, Dijon, Worcestershire, Parm, and garlic. Taste and season with salt and pepper. (You may splash the dressing with a little milk to thin it out if you'd like.) Cover and chill.

For the croutons, preheat a deep skillet over medium heat. In a bowl, toss the torn bread chunks with the oregano, a pinch each of salt and pepper, and a good drizzle of olive oil. Stir the bread in the skillet until toasted and crispy on the outside but still tender inside. Remove the croutons from the pan and allow to cool.

When you're ready to serve, cut the kale leaves away from the stems and tear into bite-size pieces. Rinse and pat or spin dry in a salad spinner. Put in a large bowl. Add the dressing and toss well. Divide the salad among serving plates or bowls. Top each salad with big shavings of Parmesan and a good handful of homemade croutons. Hit each plate with cracked black pepper to taste.

Note

I use a vegetable peeler to make nice, big Parmesan shavings!

You can absolutely substitute romaine lettuce for the kale, but kale is such a healthy choice! And it's ruffly. Ruffly makes for a pretty salad, y'all.

BLUE CHEESE WEDGE WITH MARINATED TOMATOES AND HOMEMADE HERBY RANCH

It never fails: If we go out to dinner somewhere and there's a wedge salad on the menu, I'm ordering it. With a sweet tea, please. Well, now that our kids are bigger and busier, Sam and I find ourselves at home fixing supper for two. And as sure as I order this salad when we're out, I often defer to this homemade version when we're home. What sets this wedge apart from the rest is the marinated tomatoes—such big flavor! Whether out or in, this salad's a win!

FOR THE DRESSING

1 cup mayonnaise
½ cup whole sour cream
½ cup buttermilk
2 to 3 tablespoons minced fresh dill
1 tablespoon minced fresh flat-leaf parsley
1 tablespoon minced shallot
1 garlic clove, minced
1 teaspoon Dijon mustard
1 teaspoon fresh lemon juice
Worcestershire sauce
Red pepper flakes
Salt

FOR THE SALAD

2 cups halved grape or cherry tomatoes
1 teaspoon olive oil
Balsamic vinegar
2 or 3 basil leaves, cut into chiffonade (see Note)
6 to 8 slices bacon, chopped
1 head iceberg lettuce
½ small red onion, chopped
Crumbled Stilton, Gorgonzola, or other mild blue cheese
Cracked black pepper

In a small bowl, whisk together the mayonnaise, sour cream, buttermilk, dill, parsley, shallot, garlic, Dijon, lemon juice, a dash of Worcestershire, and a few shakes of red pepper flakes. Taste and add salt or other seasoning as needed. Cover and refrigerate for 30 minutes.

In another small bowl, stir together the halved tomatoes, olive oil, a splash of balsamic vinegar, the basil chiffonade, and a pinch of salt. Set aside.

In a saucepan, sauté the chopped bacon over medium heat until nice and crispy. Transfer to a paper towel–lined plate.

When it's time to build the salads, remove the loose outer lettuce leaves and cut the head into quarters. Place each lettuce wedge on a plate. Spoon some dressing over each wedge, then top with some marinated tomatoes, crisped bacon, chopped red onion, and crumbled blue cheese. Finish with cracked black pepper.

Note

To make a chiffonade, stack a few fresh basil leaves and roll them up like a cigar. Then slice them crosswise into thin ribbons.

If your menu lends itself to needing a chopped salad, you can absolutely serve this wedge in a bowl instead! Just chop the lettuce, and toss with the ranch, tomatoes, bacon, onion, and cheese. Throw on a few homemade croutons to boot!

TOMATO, CUCUMBER, AND MOZZARELLA SALAD

This light little salad is simple to make—just a bit of chopping, a little whisking, and you're all set with a fresh, saucy bite! A zingy homemade Italian dressing really puts it over the top. I love to mix up this salad (or even double it) and send it along with my care meals because it's so portable and gets even better as it marinates in the fridge.

1 pint grape or cherry tomatoes, halved lengthwise

1 English cucumber, peeled and diced

8 ounces fresh mozzarella "pearls" (or larger mozzarella balls cut in half)

FOR THE DRESSING

5 tablespoons red wine vinegar

1 tablespoon mayonnaise

2 teaspoons honey

2 tablespoons grated Parmesan cheese

1 small garlic clove, minced

1 tablespoon minced shallot

2 teaspoons chopped fresh oregano

1 teaspoon sugar

⅓ cup olive oil

½ teaspoon salt

Ground black pepper

Red pepper flakes

Fresh basil chiffonade (see Note on page 53), for garnish

Fresh oregano leaves, for garnish

In a medium bowl, gently fold together the tomatoes, cucumber, and mozzarella.

In a small bowl, whisk together the vinegar, mayonnaise, honey, Parmesan, garlic, shallot, oregano, and sugar. Whisking vigorously, drizzle in the olive oil. Season with the salt and a pinch each of black pepper and red pepper flakes. Taste for salt and sweetness; adjust if desired. Drizzle the dressing over the tomato mixture (you may not need to use all the dressing) and gently fold the tomato mixture with the dressing. Set aside to marinate for at least 15 minutes, or up to 1 hour in the refrigerator. Garnish with basil and oregano just before serving.

GRILLED CORN AND FETA SALAD

I don't love summer. I feel sure that some of you just shrieked out loud! But y'all, being hot is one of my least favorite things to be. Just ask my family. And the humidity in the South makes my hair look all kinds of horrendous. But the produce in the summer is the best, so I endure. And I make delicious, refreshing recipes like this grilled corn salad with tomatoes and basil and a sweet, vinegary dressing. Serve it as a starter or a side, or spooned over tilapia. It looks and tastes just like summer, but without the bad hair.

4 tablespoons (½ stick) unsalted butter

¼ cup sugar

4 or 5 ears corn, shucked

1 cup halved grape or cherry tomatoes

1 shallot, chopped

3 basil leaves, cut in a chiffonade (see **Note on page 53**)

¼ cup crumbled feta cheese

½ cup olive oil

3 tablespoons rice vinegar

1 to 2 teaspoons honey or additional sugar

Salt

Fill a stockpot with water and bring to a boil over high heat. Stir in the butter and sugar. Add the corn and boil for 5 minutes. Transfer the corn to a plate and allow to air dry.

Preheat a grill pan, cast iron skillet, or outdoor grill, and grill the corn until it gets a few good, dark char marks. Transfer to the plate and set aside until cool enough to handle. When the corn has cooled, stand each ear of corn over a large plate and carefully run a knife down the cob to remove all the kernels.

In a medium bowl, combine the corn kernels, halved tomatoes, shallot, basil, and feta. In a small bowl, whisk together the oil, vinegar, honey, and a pinch of salt. Taste for seasoning and adjust. Stir the dressing into the corn mixture. Taste again for seasoning and adjust.

MEATS, MAINS, AND STURDY SOUPS

Learn little by little, meal by meal, how to feed yourself and the people you love, because food is one of the ways we love each other.
—Shauna Niequist, *Bread & Wine: A Love Letter to Life around the Table with Recipes*

GREEN CHILE AND LIME STEAK FAJITAS

Fajitas are the food of love around here. Partly because they're a crowd-pleaser but mainly because it's a meal that Sam and I prep and cook together. He is fully prepared for me to boss him a little, and I'm fully prepared for him to make a wild mess with the dry rub. For better or for worse, y'all! We double the recipe and knock out this meal for game-watching parties with friends, or we fix it as shown on any given weeknight for our family. The marinade and the rub are both winners with loads of flavor. Be sure and let the meat marinate for plenty of time. And also make sure you have a really hot cast iron skillet for your veggies! You can even switch out the steak for chicken if you'd rather. I'm willing to bet that you're gonna love this recipe like we do!

1 (2-pound) skirt steak

FOR THE MARINADE
⅔ cup canola oil
¼ cup white vinegar
Juice of 2 limes
1 (7-ounce) can diced green chiles, drained
2 garlic cloves, minced
2 teaspoons salt
1 teaspoon ground white pepper
1 teaspoon sugar
1 teaspoon granulated garlic
1 teaspoon onion powder
1 teaspoon dried oregano
1 teaspoon ground cumin

FOR THE DRY RUB
4 teaspoons chili powder
1 tablespoon brown sugar
1 tablespoon salt
1 teaspoon seasoned salt
1 teaspoon granulated garlic

(ingredients continue)

Trim the skirt steak of excess fat and put it in a large zip-top bag. In a small bowl, whisk together all the marinade ingredients. Pour the marinade into the bag with the steak, press out the air, and seal the bag. Massage the bag to coat the meat well with the marinade. Let the meat marinate in the refrigerator for at least 1 hour or as long as 4 hours.

In another small bowl, combine all the dry rub ingredients. Transfer 1 teaspoon of the mixture to a separate small bowl and reserve for the vegetables. Remove the steak from the marinade, allow the marinade to drain off, and generously season both sides of the meat with the dry rub mix.

Preheat the grill on high. When it is hot, grill the steak for 2 minutes on one side, then 2 minutes on the other side, continuing to flip and grill the steak until the internal temperature reaches 130°F for medium. Transfer the steak to a rimmed sheet pan and tent with aluminum foil for no less than 10 minutes—just the right amount of time to sauté the vegetables!

(recipe continues)

FOR THE VEGETABLES

Olive oil

1 yellow onion, sliced

1 red onion, sliced

1 yellow bell pepper, seeded and sliced into strips

1 red bell pepper, seeded and sliced into strips

1 orange bell pepper, seeded and sliced into strips

Salt

1 lime, cut in half

FOR SERVING

Flour or corn tortillas, warmed

Optional toppings: shredded Monterey Jack cheese, sour cream, sliced avocado, and chopped fresh cilantro

Heat a large cast iron skillet over medium-high heat. Drizzle a little olive oil in the bottom. When the oil is good and hot, sauté the onions and bell peppers until tender, with a little color, about 10 minutes. Season with the reserved teaspoon of dry rub, plus a few good pinches of salt. As the vegetables finish up, thinly slice the grilled skirt steak against the grain, and add the slices to the skillet. Squeeze the lime halves over the skillet and splash with a few tablespoons of water to get that restaurant sizzle!

Serve with warm tortillas and your favorite toppings.

SAM'S SMOKED PULLED PORK

This pork is perhaps the best meat on planet Earth. It's our number one go-to when we have a lot of mouths to feed—you can hop over to the Recipes that Gather chapter (page 220) to see how we build an entire crowd-feeding menu around this pork. We've estimated that over the years, we've hosted and fed this pork to around 600 people. We've served it at holidays, backyard parties, and tailgates. We've served it to football players, fraternity boys, sorority girls, and countless others. Sam has come to expect that I'll be hovering when he pulls the meat with hopes of sampling the perfect bite. In case you're wondering, this meat is cooked differently and has a different texture and flavor from the Braised Pulled Pork recipe on page 68. Both are fabulous and well worth trying!

1 (6- to 7-pound) pork shoulder (also known as Boston butt)

For the dry rub
1¼ cups white sugar
1¼ cups brown sugar
½ cup salt
¼ cup ground black pepper
¼ cup paprika
½ teaspoon cayenne pepper

Place the pork shoulder on a large rimmed sheet pan. In a medium bowl, combine all the dry rub ingredients. Use your hands to generously coat the meat on all sides. Allow the meat to marinate in the dry rub for at least 1 hour on the counter or up to 12 hours in the refrigerator. (If you choose to refrigerate it, be sure to allow the meat to sit at room temperature for at least 30 minutes before smoking it the following day.)

Preheat a smoker to 225°F. Cook the meat, fat cap up, using the indirect method specific to your smoker. Sam uses natural hardwood charcoal for the fire, and he uses hickory chips soaked in water for an hour to generate the smoke. Cook the meat for 1½ hours per pound or until the internal temperature reaches 190°F. A 7-pound pork butt usually cooks for about 10½ hours.

Line a large sheet pan with enough aluminum foil overhanging on all sides to wrap the pork shoulder. Transfer the pork to the foil-lined sheet pan and wrap well with the foil, sealing tightly. Allow the pork to rest for 30 minutes to 1 hour. Open the foil, transfer the pork to a roasting pan, and use two forks to shred the meat. Remove any large fatty parts and discard, leaving any smaller fatty parts to be mixed into the meat for flavor. And be mindful to evenly distribute the crispy bark throughout the shredded pan of meat so everyone gets a taste! Serve the meat directly out of the roasting pan or transfer to a serving dish.

(recipe continues)

Here's a handy way to calculate how many people your pork shoulder will feed: Subtract 40 percent from the raw weight of the pork shoulder to allow for shrinkage from cooking (that is, count on ending up with about 60 percent of the original weight for serving). Then multiply that number by 3 to get the number of people your pork shoulder will feed.

When making the dry rub, consider doubling or tripling the recipe for future use; store it in an airtight container. You know you're going to want to make this again!

Should your fire die before the meat has finished cooking, you may remove the meat, wrap well in foil, use a knife to cut three slits in the bottom of the foil, and finish cooking in a 225°F oven. It's best if you use a V rack in a roasting pan or on a sheet pan, lifting the meat so the drippings fall away from the meat.

Rather than trying to perfectly time the long cooking process of the meat with our serving time, Sam puts the meat in the smoker at 10 pm the night before we're planning to serve it, then he wakes to check the fire close to 6 am. If his fire went out, he will use the transfer-to-the-oven method. Otherwise, he removes the meat once it has reached 190°F, wraps it well in foil, then wraps it in a towel and places it in a small cooler until time to pull the meat for supper. The pork, wrapped and placed in a cooler, will stay warm for as long as 6 hours—it even gets better!

SALMON CROQUETTES
WITH CAJUN ALFREDO ANGEL HAIR PASTA

I first had salmon patties at my friend Cynthia McCulloch's house in Arlington, Texas, when I was in college. They changed my life. As soon as I got married, I called her and asked her to write down the recipe for me because I wanted them to become part of my arsenal. The recipe was wonderfully simple: salmon, white crackers, and eggs. Since then, I've made the recipe my own by adding other flavors and surprises (like cheese!), and they're always a hit! They're good topped with a simple lemony cream sauce, but they're positively shameful served with my homemade Cajun Alfredo sauce and pasta. Restaurant richness at home! If you're like me, you're going to find yourself eating the very first one that you take out of the pan.

FOR THE CROQUETTES

20 ounces cooked pink salmon fillets, flaked and broken up
1½ to 1¾ cups mayonnaise
2 large eggs, lightly beaten
2 cups seasoned bread crumbs
1 cup shredded mozzarella cheese
½ cup chopped green onions, plus more for garnish
Salt
Ground black pepper
Olive oil

FOR THE CAJUN ALFREDO PASTA

4 tablespoons (½ stick) unsalted butter
2 cups heavy cream
2 garlic cloves, lightly smashed
1½ cups grated Parmesan cheese, plus more for garnish
1½ teaspoons Cajun seasoning
12 ounces angel hair pasta
Chopped fresh parsley, for garnish

Set the oven to 325°F. Bring a large pot of water to a boil over high heat. Cover and have waiting.

For the croquettes, in a large bowl, combine the salmon, mayo, eggs, bread crumbs, cheese, and green onions. Season with salt and pepper to taste. Gently form patties about 2½ inches in diameter. Use a light hand to keep them plump—don't mash them down. Swirl a skillet with olive oil and heat over medium-high heat until shimmering. Cook the patties in batches for about 2 minutes on each side, or until they're nicely crisped and browned. Transfer to a wire rack set over a sheet pan. Place the croquettes in the oven to continue to warm through while you make the pasta and sauce.

In a deep saucepan, melt the butter over medium heat. Add the heavy cream and smashed garlic cloves; whisk and bring just to a boil. Lower the heat to a simmer and stir in the grated Parmesan; whisk until the Parmesan melts into the cream. Stir in the Cajun seasoning. Taste and adjust. Spoon out the garlic cloves and discard.

Meanwhile, add the angel hair pasta to the pot of boiling water and cook just until al dente, about 4 minutes. Drain the pasta, add to the pan with the Alfredo sauce, and toss well to coat.

Divide the Cajun Alfredo pasta among shallow serving bowls and top each with 3 salmon croquettes. Sprinkle with extra Parm, chopped green onions, and parsley.

G-DAD'S PORK TENDERLOIN WITH PARMESAN-GARLIC CREAM

My daddy loves to cook. He's the one who ventures out and tries a new recipe right out of a cookbook or one that he's come across online. He has a few recipes that are his favorites to fix when we come home to visit, and this is one of them. We all love it. When my kids were little, they began referring to it as "G-Dad's Tenderloin," and that's what we call it to this day! The marinade and cream sauce are mostly his, with just a few adjustments that I've snuck in. This is a recipe that your friends and family will rave about, and you'll be delighted that it was so simple. But you don't have to tell them—your secret's safe with me.

FOR THE CREAM SAUCE

¾ **cup mayonnaise**
¾ **cup whole sour cream**
1 **tablespoon Dijon mustard**
1 **teaspoon Worcestershire sauce**
2 **tablespoons grated Parmesan cheese**
1 **tablespoon (heaping) minced garlic**
½ **teaspoon salt**
Ground black pepper to taste

FOR THE TENDERLOINS

2 **(1¼-pound) pork tenderloins**
2 **cups vegetable oil**
⅓ **cup soy sauce**
¼ **cup honey**
1 **tablespoon minced shallot**
1 **tablespoon minced garlic**
Salt
Ground black pepper
Chopped fresh chives, for garnish

In a small bowl, whisk together all the cream sauce ingredients. Cover and refrigerate.

Use a sharp knife to carefully trim the silverskin from the tenderloins. Remove any excess fat. Place the tenderloins in a large zip-top bag. In a small bowl, whisk together the vegetable oil, soy sauce, honey, shallot, and garlic. Pour the marinade into the bag with the meat, press out the air, and seal the bag. Massage the bag to coat the tenderloins well with the marinade. Let the meat marinate in the refrigerator for at least 4 hours.

Set the oven to 400°F.

Remove the tenderloins from the bag, gently pat off the excess marinade with paper towels, and generously salt and pepper all sides. Heat a large cast iron skillet over medium-high heat. Sear all sides of the tenderloins to get a good dark crust. Transfer the tenderloins to a baking dish and bake for 15 minutes, or until the internal temperature reaches 145°F. Perfect pork is a little pink! Tent the tenderloins with aluminum foil and allow to rest for about 10 minutes before slicing into medallions. While the pork is in the oven, remove the cream sauce from the refrigerator and allow it to come to room temperature.

Spoon the cream sauce over the pork medallions and garnish with chopped chives.

BRAISED PULLED PORK

There are two pulled pork recipes in this book, and for good reason: They're both irresistible! Sam's Smoked Pulled Pork (page 63) is a drier meat cooked in a smoker, with a delicious bark like the meat found in BBQ joints. This braised pulled pork is wetter, saucier, and spicier. It's also doable in a shorter amount of time and is cooked in the oven rather than outside. If you're lucky, you'll have a little left over for tacos or a plate of nachos. Some nights after we've served this dish to company, they've gone home, and the kitchen is clean, Sam and I give each other a high five. Full bellies and full hearts deserve high fives in our book.

FOR THE DRY RUB

½ **cup brown sugar**
⅓ **cup salt**
1 **teaspoon onion powder**
1 **teaspoon granulated garlic**
1 **teaspoon ground cumin**
1 **teaspoon chili powder**
1 **teaspoon dried oregano**
1 **teaspoon dry mustard**
½ **teaspoon red pepper flakes**

FOR THE PORK

1 **(3½-pound) bone-in pork shoulder (also known as Boston butt)**
Olive oil
2 **yellow onions, quartered**
2 **(32-ounce) cartons beef stock**
3 **tablespoons apple cider vinegar**
Liquid smoke

FOR SERVING

Texas toast or hamburger buns
BBQ sauce
Pickled Chow-Chow (page 50)
Sliced red onion

Set the oven to 325°F.

In a small bowl, combine all the dry rub ingredients. Pat the pork dry with paper towels and allow the meat to sit at room temperature for 20 minutes or so. Coat the meat all over with the dry rub, pressing it into the crevices and into the meat. Be generous.

Heat a Dutch oven over medium-high heat. Drizzle a little olive oil in the bottom, then use kitchen tongs to sear the meat on all sides until well browned. Don't skip this step or cut it short—a good dark crust on the outside of the meat means big flavor! When the pork is seared well on all sides, tuck the quartered onions around the sides of the meat. Pour in enough stock to nearly cover the meat, lifting it a little with the tongs so the stock can get underneath it. Add the apple cider vinegar and a dash of liquid smoke. Bring the liquid just to a boil, then cover with a tight-fitting lid and put in the oven for 3½ to 4 hours. The pork is ready when the bone jiggles out easily or when a fork can easily pull the meat apart.

Transfer the pork to a deep serving platter or tray and pull apart the meat with two forks. Spoon a little of the braising liquid over the meat and stir in the cooked onions if you'd like. Serve open-face on toasted Texas toast or on classic buns with BBQ sauce, chow-chow, and thick slices of red onion.

SIGNATURE SHRIMP AND GRITS

You know that special dish you make when you want to serve something impressive, memorable, and divinely delicious? Well, this is mine, and I'm willing to bet it may become yours, too! It's a crowd-pleaser—just ask the gals who lick their bowls and the fellas who hug my neck after they eat this meal at my house. This dish has become my signature because I've made it for everyone on God's green Earth. And you know what? They ask for it again and again. The shrimp sauce is spicy and sweet, the grits (my sister-in-law Allison's recipe) are cheesy, creamy, and garlicky, and then I top off each bowl with salty, smoky bacon. Oh my word!

FOR THE SHRIMP

1 tablespoon unsalted butter

1 teaspoon olive oil

1½ pounds large raw shrimp (41–50 per pound), peeled and deveined, tails left on

Creole seasoning

6 slices thick-cut hickory bacon, chopped

FOR THE CHEESE GRITS

2 cups water

2 cups milk

8 tablespoons (1 stick) unsalted butter

½ teaspoon salt

1 cup quick 5-minute grits

1 pound Mild Mexican Velveeta, diced

1 teaspoon granulated garlic

3 tablespoons jarred chopped jalapeños and juice

(ingredients continue)

In a large skillet with a lid, heat the butter and oil over medium heat. Lay the shrimp in the pan in a single layer, dust with a bit of Creole seasoning, and cook on both sides for a minute or two. The shrimp are done when the tails are red and the flesh is barely white. Transfer the shrimp to a plate and tent them with aluminum foil to keep warm.

In the same skillet, sauté the chopped bacon over medium heat until crisp and nicely browned. Using a slotted spoon or spatula, transfer the bacon pieces to a paper towel–lined plate, reserving the bacon grease in the skillet. Turn off the burner, but leave the skillet where it is.

In a medium saucepan, bring the water, milk, butter, and salt to a boil over medium heat. Whisk in the grits, whisking constantly so they do not clump. Reduce the heat to a simmer and cook the grits until they've expanded and gotten creamy, 7 to 8 minutes. Over low heat, stir in the cheese and granulated garlic until the cheese is melted and the grits are smooth. Stir in the jarred jalapeños and juice. Taste as you go! Add more milk or butter a little at a time, stirring over low heat until the grits are creamy, creamy, creamy.

Meanwhile, heat the bacon grease over medium heat, add the peppers and onion, and sauté for 3 to 4 minutes, or until they are tender but not soft. Add the chopped garlic and stir constantly for 1 minute to be sure it doesn't burn—and it will burn on you fast. Add the wine and allow it to cook for a minute, then stir in

(recipe continues)

FOR THE SAUCE

1 red bell pepper, seeded and
 chopped
1 yellow bell pepper, seeded and
 chopped
1 yellow onion, chopped
2 garlic cloves, chopped
½ cup dry white wine
1½ cups unsalted chicken stock
1½ tablespoons Creole
 seasoning
Juice of 1 lemon

FOR GARNISH

2 to 3 tablespoons chopped
 green onions (green parts
 only)
Crumbled goat cheese (optional)
Crusty bread, for serving

the stock and the Creole seasoning. Cover the skillet and allow the sauce to simmer for several minutes while you stir the grits. Remove the lid from the sauce, stir in the sautéed shrimp, and squeeze in the lemon juice. Allow the shrimp to warm back up a little in the sauce. Taste, adding more Creole seasoning, more lemon juice, or more wine or stock if you prefer.

To serve, spoon the creamy jalapeño cheese grits into shallow bowls and ladle the shrimp and sauce on top. Garnish with the crumbled bacon, chopped green onions, and a crumble of goat cheese if you'd like. I like to lay a hunk of rustic crusty bread on the side of each bowl for moppin' up every last bit of grits and sauce from the bowl.

Note

Whatever you do, don't buy instant grits. They are not the same as quick 5-minute grits. Be mindful that you get the right ones!

FAJITA GUACAMOLE BURGERS

When we have friends over on a pretty night, we love to grill—but we often find ourselves tug-of-warring over burgers versus fajitas. The all-American burger is hard to beat, but fajitas with caramelized peppers and onions and other beloved toppings call to us! So I created this recipe to deliver everything we crave about our two favorite grill-out meals. These perfectly seasoned burgers are sauced with a creamy avocado spread, then piled with pepper Jack cheese and sautéed peppers and onions. This recipe will make you want to sweep the patio, light the citronellas, and call your neighbors!

FOR THE PATTIES
2 pounds ground beef (80% lean)
2 teaspoons Worcestershire sauce

FOR THE GUACAMOLE SPREAD
3 ripe avocados
¾ cup quartered cherry or grape tomatoes
Juice of 1 lime
1 teaspoon (heaping) whole sour cream
½ teaspoon ground cumin
½ teaspoon granulated garlic
Hot sauce
Salt

FOR THE TACO SEASONING
4 teaspoons chili powder
2 teaspoons cumin
2 teaspoons salt
1 teaspoon black pepper
1 teaspoon brown sugar
½ teaspoon onion powder
½ teaspoon granulated garlic
½ teaspoon dried oregano
¼ teaspoon cayenne pepper

(ingredients continue)

Put the ground beef in a medium bowl and use your hands to mix in the Worcestershire. Gently form 6 patties about ¾ inch thick, and use your thumb to make an indention in the middle of each patty to help your burgers grill flat. Lay the patties on a parchment-lined sheet pan and refrigerate them while you continue to work.

To make the guacamole spread, halve the avocados, remove the pits, and scoop the avocado flesh into a bowl. Use a fork to mash it well. Stir in the tomatoes, lime juice, sour cream, cumin, garlic, and a dash of hot sauce, then season with salt to taste. Cover the guacamole with plastic wrap, gently pressing it directly onto the surface of the guacamole to keep it from browning; refrigerate.

Preheat the grill on high.

In a small bowl, combine all the ingredients for the taco seasoning. Season the patties generously with the taco seasoning, reserving 1 teaspoon of the seasoning for the peppers and onions.

Grill the patties for 3 to 5 minutes per side. Transfer to a sheet pan, pile some shredded pepper Jack cheese on each, then tent with aluminum foil.

(recipe continues)

**2 cups shredded pepper Jack
cheese**

Olive oil

**1 yellow bell pepper, seeded and
sliced into strips**

**1 red bell pepper, seeded and
sliced into strips**

**1 orange bell pepper, seeded
and sliced into strips**

**1 large yellow onion, halved
and sliced**

**6 good hamburger buns, buttered
and toasted**

Meanwhile, swirl a cast iron skillet with a little olive oil and heat over medium-high heat until shimmering. Sauté the pepper and onion strips until tender, with a little color, 5 to 7 minutes. Season with the reserved teaspoon of taco seasoning.

To build the burgers, spread guacamole on each toasted bottom bun, followed by a cheesy patty, some sautéed peppers and onions, and a toasted top bun.

BRAISED CARNE ASADA TACOS

I love to cook. Period. But what really thrills my soul is cooking a meal that I know someone especially loves. This braised carne asada is my son Isaac's favorite. He asks for it when he has friends over or when we're having a special meal in his honor to celebrate his birthday, good grades, making the state tournament, or returning home from a trip of some kind. The meat with its spicy rub is mouthwatering, and the peppers and onions turn into delicious mush, soaking up all the flavors in the pot. We pile it all on warm flour tortillas and top with sliced avocado, sour cream, and shredded Monterey Jack or a Mexican crumbling cheese. Then we stand in the kitchen and nibble any leftover meat with our fingers until we nearly pop!

FOR THE DRY RUB

4 teaspoons chili powder
2 teaspoons ground cumin
2 teaspoons salt
1 teaspoon ground black pepper
1 teaspoon brown sugar
½ teaspoon onion powder
½ teaspoon granulated garlic
½ teaspoon dried oregano
¼ teaspoon cayenne pepper

FOR THE BEEF

2 pounds flank or skirt steak
Olive oil
½ cup + 1½ cups beef stock
2 yellow onions, halved and sliced
1 red bell pepper, seeded and cut into strips
1 yellow bell pepper, seeded and cut into strips

In a small bowl, combine the ingredients for the dry rub. Set aside.

Allow the beef to sit at room temperature for 10 minutes, then use a meat mallet to pound the meat a little to break down the connective tissue and tenderize it. Cut the meat in half so it will fit in your pot if necessary.

Set the oven to 325°F.

Rub both sides of the meat liberally with the dry rub. Swirl a little oil in an oven-safe stockpot, Dutch oven, or enameled braiser and heat over medium-high heat until shimmering. Sear the meat on both sides until a dark crust forms. (If you had to cut the meat in half to fit in your pan, then sear in batches.) Transfer the meat to a plate.

Pour in ½ cup stock, stirring to loosen the browned bits on the bottom of the pan. Then add the onions and peppers, stirring to cook for a few minutes. Push the veggies to the sides to make a center spot for the meat. Lay the meat in the pan, nestling it down between the vegetables. Pour in the remaining 1½ cups stock. The stock should come up the sides of the meat without covering the top. Cover the pan and bake for 2½ hours. Turn off the oven and continue to cook (without peeking) for another 30 to 60 minutes. Remove from the oven, and shred the meat in the pan with two forks, stirring the shredded meat and vegetables together in the pan juices. The meat should pull apart easily. If the meat doesn't shred into tender bites, cover the pan and return it to the oven for 30 minutes more.

CHILI AND BROWN SUGAR PORK CHOPS WITH PAN GRAVY

I had a Great Uncle Buddy who was a big, burly teddy bear of a man. He used to flavor up his flour with paprika and sugar when he made pork chops, and my mama started doing the same when she fixed pork chops for us at home. And now I'm continuing the tradition when I make them for my own family. This breading is a little bit sweet with brown sugar and a little bit spicy with chili powder, but it all becomes delightfully savory when it's skillet fried and then baked in the oven. And then there's the gravy—my word! *Please* promise me you'll make homemade mashed potatoes with these chops. It would be a sin not to.

- 1 cup all-purpose flour
- 3 tablespoons brown sugar
- 3 teaspoons salt, plus more for seasoning
- 2 teaspoons chili powder
- ½ teaspoon granulated garlic
- 2 large eggs
- 4 (¾- to 1-inch-thick) bone-in pork chops
- Vegetable oil
- 1 tablespoon bacon grease or unsalted butter
- 4 cups milk
- Ground black pepper
- Gruyère Mashed Potatoes (page 139), for serving
- Chopped fresh parsley, for garnish (optional)

Set the oven to 375°F. Heat a large cast iron skillet over medium heat.

Combine the flour, brown sugar, salt, chili powder, and granulated garlic in a pie plate or shallow dish. Measure out ¼ cup of the flour mixture and set it aside for the gravy. In another pie plate or shallow dish, whisk the eggs. Lightly salt both sides of each pork chop, dredge in the egg wash on both sides, then coat in the flour mixture on both sides. Make sure all parts of the meat are coated in the flour mixture.

When all four pork chops are dredged and coated, swirl the preheated skillet with a little vegetable oil. When the oil is hot, crisp each pork chop until the coating is golden brown, about 2 minutes on each side. It's important to note two things here: First, this step is not intended to cook the chops through; it's intended to get a yummy crust on the outside. Second, you are going to use all the good stuff in the bottom of this pan for the gravy base, so don't wash it out! When the chops have developed a good golden crust, remove the skillet from the heat and transfer the chops to a wire rack set over a sheet pan. Bake for 7 to 10 minutes, or until the internal temperature reaches 145°F.

Now, return the skillet to medium-low heat; it should have a little leftover grease and some crumbles from the pork chops. That's flavor! Melt the bacon grease or butter in the pan, then shake in the reserved ¼ cup flour mixture. Using a fork or a whisk, stir the flour into the pan goodness and bacon grease to form a lovely brown paste. Pour in the milk and whisk. Increase the heat to medium and bring just to a boil; then reduce to a simmer, whisking often. The gravy will thicken in only a few minutes as it simmers. Season with salt and pepper to taste.

To serve, place a pork chop in the center of each plate, heap a scoop of mashed potatoes on top, then ladle the whole pile with gravy. Season with black pepper and garnish with chopped parsley, if you're feeling fancy.

SPICY COFFEE-RUBBED STRIP STEAKS
WITH SMOKED PAPRIKA AND GARLIC BUTTER

Gosh, we love steak. And it's because of recipes like this that Sam and I would rather cook our own steak dinner at home than go out. All you need is a good cast iron skillet, quality meat, and flavor-infused butter. These strip steaks are rubbed in a rich, spicy seasoning blend, sizzled in a cast iron skillet to get a crust like no other, then finished off for just a few minutes in a hot oven. What truly puts them over the top is a shamefully good drizzle of paprika butter. This recipe can easily be adjusted to fix as many steaks as your skillet can sear!

FOR THE STEAKS
4 (10-ounce) New York strip steaks
1 K-cup (5 teaspoons) strong ground coffee
4 teaspoons brown sugar
4 teaspoons granulated garlic
4 teaspoons smoked paprika
4 teaspoons salt
4 teaspoons ground black pepper
2 teaspoons red pepper flakes
Olive oil

FOR THE PAPRIKA BUTTER
6 tablespoons unsalted butter
3 garlic cloves, lightly smashed
Juice of 1 small lemon
1 teaspoon smoked paprika
Salt
1 tablespoon finely chopped fresh flat-leaf parsley

Pat the steaks dry, lay them in a single layer on a sheet pan, and refrigerate, uncovered, for several hours.

In a small bowl, combine the coffee, brown sugar, granulated garlic, smoked paprika, salt, black pepper, and red pepper flakes. Remove the steaks from the refrigerator, rub with a small amount of olive oil, and season both sides generously with the dry rub. Allow to sit at room temperature for an hour so the seasoning can soak in and flavor the meat.

Preheat the oven to 500°F.

In a small saucepan, melt the butter over medium-low heat. Add the smashed garlic and stir until fragrant. Reduce the heat to keep the butter warm, and stir in the lemon juice, smoked paprika, and a pinch of salt.

Preheat a heavy cast iron skillet on high heat. Sear the steaks for 1 to 2 minutes per side to get a good crust. Transfer the steaks to a wire rack set over a sheet pan and finish cooking in the oven for 3 to 5 minutes, or until the internal temperature reaches your desired doneness (about 140°F for medium; keep in mind that the temperature will rise another 5 to 10 degrees as the steaks rest). Tent the steaks with aluminum foil and allow to rest for 10 minutes before serving.

Plate the steaks. Remove the garlic from the butter and discard, then stir in the parsley. Drizzle the warm flavored butter over the steaks.

SWEET RED PEPPER SHRIMP TACOS
WITH PUFFY SHELLS

Bonnie's Red Pepper Jelly is a best seller in my store. I put it on everything from soft cream cheese to Christmas ham. And it was my love for red pepper jelly that resulted in these shrimp tacos. Y'all, they are outstanding—think bang bang with less grease and more flavor! We heap on the honey-cilantro slaw to balance the sweet heat from the red pepper sauce, but it's so good we love it even forked on the side. These tacos are saucy, sloppy, and spectacular, and you won't believe how easy they are to make. It's restaurant quality at home!

FOR THE SWEET RED PEPPER SAUCE

⅓ cup mayonnaise

¼ cup red pepper jelly

1 teaspoon chili sauce

½ teaspoon Sriracha sauce

½ teaspoon cayenne pepper

¼ teaspoon granulated garlic

¼ teaspoon red pepper flakes, plus more for serving

FOR THE SLAW

¾ cup mayonnaise

¼ cup apple cider vinegar

3 tablespoons honey

Juice of 1 lime

¼ cup chopped fresh cilantro, plus more for serving

½ teaspoon sugar

¼ teaspoon salt

8 cups shredded napa cabbage

FOR THE SHRIMP TACOS

Vegetable oil

1 pound large raw shrimp (41–50 per pound), peeled, deveined, and tails removed

8 (6-inch) flour tortillas

8 ounces shredded Monterey Jack cheese

Lime wedges, for serving

Sliced avocado, for serving

In a small bowl, whisk together all the ingredients for the sweet red pepper sauce. Set aside.

In a large bowl, whisk together all the ingredients for the slaw dressing, then toss in the green cabbage. Set aside.

Swirl a bit of vegetable oil in a medium saucepan, then sauté the shrimp over medium heat for about 1 minute. Stir in the sweet red pepper sauce, lower the heat to medium-low, and sauté until the shrimp have cooked through and the sauce has reduced, about 3 minutes. Remove from the heat.

Pour vegetable oil into a cast iron skillet to a depth of about ¾ inch. Heat over medium heat until it shimmers. Use long tongs to fry the flour tortillas for about a minute on each side. The tortillas will puff up, breathe a little, and turn a light golden brown. Drain on a paper towel–lined sheet pan.

To serve, spoon several shrimp with sauce into each puffy tortilla and pile with slaw and shredded cheese. Serve with lime wedges, avocado slices, additional red pepper flakes, and cilantro.

HATCH GREEN CHILE PATTY MELTS

This recipe is a delicious spin on a classic patty melt—peppery sweet from the Hatch green chiles and spicy from the Creole seasoning. My boys love them, their friends love them, and I love them. This recipe makes four sandwiches, but they're so rich and loaded that they'll easily feed six or eight. Cut them on the diagonal and dunk them in the tangy cream sauce.

6 tablespoons unsalted butter, plus more for grilling the sandwiches
1 large red onion, thinly sliced
1 large yellow onion, thinly sliced
Salt
1½ pounds ground beef (80% lean)
1 (4-ounce) can chopped Hatch green chiles, drained
Worcestershire sauce
Creole seasoning
1 cup mayonnaise
Juice of 1 lemon
2 tablespoons chopped fresh dill
1 small shallot, minced
1 garlic clove, minced
Red pepper flakes
8 slices sturdy sandwich bread, like farmhouse white or sourdough
2 cups shredded Monterey Jack cheese
2 cups shredded medium cheddar cheese

Preheat a large cast iron skillet over medium heat, then melt the butter just until it begins to foam. Add the onions and a pinch or two of salt and sauté for several minutes. Reduce the heat to medium-low and allow the onions to caramelize for 20 minutes or so, stirring occasionally, while you prep the burgers and sauce.

Meanwhile, in a large bowl, gently combine the ground beef, chiles, and a few dashes of Worcestershire. Try to incorporate the chiles without mashing the meat. Divide into four sections and carefully press them out into large, thin patties. Place the patties on a parchment-lined sheet pan. Generously sprinkle Creole seasoning over the tops of the patties. Place the sheet pan in the refrigerator for 10 minutes, or until it's time to cook the burgers.

In a small bowl, combine the mayonnaise, lemon juice, dill, shallot, garlic, and a pinch of red pepper flakes. Stir, cover, and refrigerate until time to serve.

Preheat another skillet over medium-high heat, and swirl 2 or 3 tablespoons of butter in the bottom. Brown the patties for about 2 minutes per side. Cook without lifting them, allowing a good crust to form. Gently press the center down so they don't puff up in the middle. The patties should still be a little pink in the center when they're done. Transfer to a wire rack set over a sheet pan. Carefully wipe out the skillet with paper towels and return it to the stove. Melt another 2 or 3 tablespoons of butter in the skillet.

To build the patty melts, layer a slice of bread, some cheese, a patty, some onions, more cheese, and another slice of bread. Grill each patty melt in the skillet swirled with butter, pressing down to keep the sandwich together. Grill on both sides until the cheese is melted and the bread is toasty. Repeat with all four sandwiches, adding more butter to the skillet as necessary. Serve with the tangy cream sauce.

SUNDAY RED BEANS AND RICE

I know all my people's favorites. And nothing tickles me more than fixing a dish that I know someone special will love. My preacher hubby loves red beans and rice; it's his flavor profile of choice. Earthy, smoky, savory, and spicy, with a good roux base. So when he's had a busy week, a big something, or just because I love him so, I stir up this recipe. It's become the perfect comfort meal for me to make for him on Sundays after he's preached all morning. Food speaks love. And it doesn't hurt that it's the easiest recipe on God's green Earth.

2 pounds smoked sausage or kielbasa, sliced

4 to 6 slices bacon, chopped

1 orange bell pepper, seeded and chopped

½ yellow onion, chopped

2 or 3 garlic cloves, chopped

¼ cup flour

3 (14-ounce) cans red beans, partially drained

1 cup beef stock, plus more if needed

1 to 2 teaspoons Creole seasoning

½ teaspoon salt

2 cups cooked white rice

Preheat a deep skillet or braiser over medium heat. Cook the sausage rounds until slightly browned, then transfer to a plate and cover to keep warm. Add the bacon and sauté until crisp. Use a slotted spoon to transfer the bacon to a paper towel–lined plate, reserving the fat in the pan. Turn the heat to low and add the bell pepper, onion, and garlic and sauté in the bacon fat just until tender. Shake the flour over the vegetables; cook and stir for a few minutes. Pour in the beans and stock and then add the Creole seasoning and salt. Stir to combine. Simmer, stirring occasionally, until thickened. Return the sausage and bacon to the pan. Taste for seasoning and adjust. Stir in the cooked rice.

Note

Pair a bowl of red beans and rice with my Salmon Croquettes (page 66), and you'll think you've gone to Heaven.

WHITE CHICKEN CHILI
WITH CILANTRO AND LIME

This is an adaptation of a recipe found in my church cookbook that was submitted by Babs Carter. Y'all know that if you can ever get your hands on a church cookbook, then it's a keeper. Church cookbook recipes are those tried-and-true, time-tested, crowd-pleasing dishes. I know, because I'm a pastor's wife, and I've been feeding people for more than 20 years. So you learn what's good, what people come back for, and what they request recipes for. And this chili meets the criteria for sure! It is loaded with flavor, and the texture is divine—creamy but with bites of tender chicken and white beans. Topped with thin slices of avocado and a dollop of sour cream . . . mmmmm! You and your people are going to love it!

2 tablespoons olive oil

2 cups chopped yellow onion

5 garlic cloves, chopped

1 tablespoon dried oregano

2 teaspoons ground cumin

1 teaspoon ground ginger

3 cups chicken stock

½ cup dry white wine or additional chicken stock

1 bay leaf, broken in half

3 cups shredded cooked chicken

3 (14-ounce) cans white beans, rinsed and drained

3 jalapeño peppers, minced

3 cups grated Monterey Jack cheese

½ teaspoon ground black pepper

Salt

Juice of 3 limes

3 tablespoons chopped fresh cilantro, plus more for topping

Optional toppings: chopped fresh tomatoes, chopped green onions, sliced avocado, sour cream, and shredded Monterey Jack cheese

Heat the olive oil in a large, heavy pot or Dutch oven over medium heat. Add the onion and sauté until tender and just starting to get color. Add the garlic, oregano, cumin, and ginger and cook for another minute. Stir continuously so the garlic doesn't burn! Add the stock, wine (if using), and bay leaf. Cook for 5 minutes, or until somewhat reduced. Stir in the chicken, beans, and jalapeños. Simmer for 10 minutes, stirring occasionally.

Turn the heat down to low and add the cheese, a little at a time, stirring until melted. Add the pepper and taste; add salt if needed. Stir in the lime juice and chopped cilantro and simmer for 5 minutes. Remove the bay leaf halves before serving with all your favorite toppings.

Note

A few shortcuts can make this recipe an even bigger winner: Use deli rotisserie chicken and chopped jalapeños from a jar!

Resist the urge to buy pre-shredded cheese and just shred your own! It'll melt beautifully into the stock for the *best* chili ever!

BROWN SUGAR CHILI
OVER CHEESE GRITS

We love to gather all kinds of folks for all kinds of reasons at our house. Couples, teenagers, college students, our kids' friends, our kids' friends' families, neighbors—you name it. We always have an open door and an open fridge. Most of our gatherings are casual and easy and filling in every way. I often serve this hearty chili and grits to large groups. The cheese grits stretch the recipe and fill bellies faster than chili alone. Good food and good company. Full hearts and full bellies. It's what I'm all about!

FOR THE BROWN SUGAR CHILI

Olive oil

1 small yellow onion, chopped

2 garlic cloves, chopped

2 pounds ground beef (80% lean)

1 (14-ounce) can dark red kidney beans, partially drained

1 (14-ounce) can light red kidney beans, partially drained

1 (14-ounce) can pinto beans, partially drained

1 (14-ounce) can black beans, partially drained

2 (10-ounce) cans diced tomatoes with green chiles

1 (4-ounce) can chopped green chiles

1 (4-ounce) can tomato paste

1 (1.25-ounce) packet chili seasoning

1 (1-ounce) packet ranch dressing mix

2 to 3 tablespoons brown sugar

Salt

Ground black pepper

Note

Cheese Grits page 71

In a large heavy pot, swirl a bit of olive oil. Add the onion and sauté over medium heat until tender. Stir in the garlic and sauté until fragrant. Add the ground beef and cook, breaking it up with your spoon, until browned. Add all the beans to the pot. Pour in the tomatoes and chiles with their juice. Add the tomato paste, chili seasoning, ranch dressing mix, brown sugar, and salt and pepper to taste. Stir well. Bring just to a boil, reduce to low, and simmer for 30 minutes. Add a can of water if you prefer your chili more liquidy than thick.

Prepare the cheese grits from the Signature Shrimp and Grits recipe on page 71. Ladle just enough grits into each shallow bowl to cover the bottom, then fill with chili. Garnish with whatever toppings sound good!

HEARTY HOMEMADE CHICKEN AND DUMPLINS

This classic chicken and dumplins recipe is as rich and warm and filling as it gets. I'm not teasing you—my family *Mmmmms* the whole time they eat a bowl of this goodness. I love making it. The process is therapeutic and makes me feel a heart-connection to days gone by, especially when I make my own stock. Chicken and dumplins is perfect to serve on those early dark nights when the weather turns colder and the wind is stirring the leaves out the window and you're in sock-feet. It's rib-sticking comfort in a bowl.

FOR THE CHICKEN

3 tablespoons + 2 tablespoons unsalted butter
1 cup chopped yellow onion
1 cup chopped carrot
1 cup chopped celery
¼ cup all-purpose flour
2 (32-ounce) cartons chicken stock
Salt
Ground black pepper
4 cups shredded cooked chicken
Leaves from several fresh thyme sprigs

FOR THE DUMPLINS

2 cups all-purpose flour, plus more for sprinkling
2 teaspoons baking powder
1 teaspoon salt
⅓ cup vegetable shortening (such as Crisco)
½ cup cold whole milk

In a large, heavy pot or Dutch oven, melt 3 tablespoons butter over low heat. Add the onion, carrot, and celery and sauté until tender. Shake the flour over the veggies; cook and stir for about 2 minutes to cook out the raw flour taste. Pour in the chicken stock, stir, and bring to a boil over medium heat.

Meanwhile, to make the dumplins, whisk together the flour, baking powder, and salt in a large bowl. Add the shortening and roll it around to cover it in flour. Then with your fingers, break apart the shortening into pea-size pieces, tossing them in the flour and incorporating them well. Make a well in the middle of the mixture and add the cold milk. Using a spoon, stir to make a stiff dough. It will be messy looking and not smooth.

Lightly flour your work surface and turn out the dough. Gather the dough into a ball and gently knead it five or six times, being careful not to overwork the dough. Lightly flour a rolling pin and roll out the dough to about ¼-inch thickness, adding a light dusting of flour to your dough or your pin if needed. The dough will be craggy, and that's okay. Using a rolling pizza cutter or knife, cut 1-inch squares or diamonds in the dough. Use a spatula or bench scraper to scoop up all the dumplins, plus all the extra flour, and add them to the boiling stock. Stir to make sure they don't stick together. Add a good pinch each of salt and pepper. Cover the pot, leaving a little crack, and boil gently over medium heat for 8 to 10 minutes. Carefully open the lid, stir in the shredded chicken and remaining 2 tablespoons butter, and continue to simmer on low for another 8 to 10 minutes, or until it is the desired thickness. Add the fresh thyme and season with salt and pepper to taste.

CREAMY PESTO TORTELLINI SOUP

This is my friend Beth's staple care meal that she takes to friends who need the comfort and ministry of food for whatever reason. I was at her house one afternoon sitting at her table when she stirred this up for a mom of four who had pneumonia, and she let me have a little bite. It's simple and quick—and y'all, sometimes recipes need to be simple and quick so that nothing stands in the way of hospitality! It's no wonder why it's Beth's go-to. And it's a convenient weeknight supper for your people, too!

1 tablespoon unsalted butter

1 small yellow onion, chopped

1 garlic clove, minced

1 (32-ounce) carton chicken stock

1 (15-ounce) jar Alfredo sauce

3 cups shredded rotisserie chicken

1 (20-ounce) bag refrigerated cheese tortellini

5 tablespoons pesto

Chopped fresh basil, for garnish

Grated Parmesan cheese, for garnish

In a large Dutch oven or soup pot, melt the butter over medium heat. Add the onion and sauté for several minutes, or until tender. Add the garlic and stir for about 1 minute, just until fragrant. Stir in the chicken stock and Alfredo sauce. Add the chicken and bring to a boil. Add the tortellini and cook according to the package direction, usually only a few minutes. Stir in the pesto. Ladle into bowls and garnish with basil and freshly grated Parmesan cheese.

Note

The tortellini will continue to expand even after they've cooked for the proper amount of time, so add them to the soup only when you're about to serve it! If you're traveling this soup to someone who needs to be loved with food, I suggest not adding the tortellini. Along with the pot of soup, send the unopened bag of tortellini with instructions for bringing the soup back to a boil and then adding the tortellini just before they wish to eat it. This ensures that the tortellini hold their shape and are their best at mealtime!

No. 4

COMFORTS AND CASSEROLES

The act of sharing a meal and talking about God is one
of the best ways I know to do life together.
—Susie Davis

COTTAGE PIE
WITH PUFF PASTRY

If you took everything comforting and layered it in a casserole dish, you'd get this cottage pie. Traditionally, a cottage pie is any kind of meat topped with mashed potatoes. But this recipe goes farther: meat, veggies, a yummy sauce, cream cheese mashed potatoes, a cheese layer, and a salted puff pastry right on top. Every bite has something to love! There are lots of ingredients but not very many steps, so don't let the list intimidate you! Think of a chilly night when everything gets canceled unexpectedly, and you're tucked inside your home with this comfort meal and your people all in sweaters and socks. There's nothing better for your soul than hospitality at home.

For the mashed potatoes

- 1¾ pounds petite Yukon Gold potatoes, quartered
- 1 teaspoon salt, plus more for seasoning
- ½ cup heavy cream, plus more if needed
- ½ cup chicken stock
- 4 tablespoons (½ stick) unsalted butter
- ½ (4-ounce) package cream cheese
- Ground black pepper

For the filling

- 1½ pounds ground beef (80% lean)
- 1 medium onion, chopped
- 2 garlic cloves, chopped
- 1 cup diced carrot
- 1 cup frozen peas
- ¼ cup all-purpose flour
- 2 cups good beef stock
- 2 tablespoons tomato paste
- Salt
- Ground black pepper
- 1 tablespoon minced fresh rosemary
- ½ cup shredded white cheddar cheese
- 1 sheet frozen puff pastry, thawed

Put the potatoes in a large pot and cover them with cold water by about 2 inches. Add 1 teaspoon salt. Cover the pot and bring to a boil over medium-high heat, then reduce to a simmer and cook the potatoes for 15 to 20 minutes, or until fork-tender and the skin is starting to come loose.

While the potatoes are boiling, combine the cream, stock, and butter in a small saucepan; warm over low heat. Drain the potatoes, return to the pot, and pour in the warmed cream mixture, stirring in the softened cream cheese. Carefully mash with a potato masher, stirring and mashing until partly chunky and partly creamy. Salt and pepper well to taste. Let stand while you prepare the beef mixture.

Set the oven to 375°F.

In a large skillet, brown the ground beef with the onion over medium heat. Spoon out and discard about half of the fat. Add the garlic and carrots; stir until fragrant and becoming tender. Stir in the frozen peas. Shake the flour over the mixture and stir well. Stir in the beef stock; it should just cover the mixture. Stir in the tomato paste. Season generously with salt and pepper and stir well, allowing the liquid to simmer and thicken just a little. Stir in the rosemary. Taste for seasoning and adjust. Spoon the beef mixture into a deep, round casserole dish.

Remove the lid from the potatoes and mash and stir them until creamier but still a little chunky, adding more cream if needed to get them to a spreadable consistency. Season generously with salt and pepper. Taste for seasoning and adjust.

Carefully spread the mashed potatoes over the meat mixture in the casserole dish. Sprinkle the shredded white cheddar all over the top. Cover with the thawed puff pastry. Cut several slits in the pastry to vent steam. Brush the pastry with a little extra cream, and salt and pepper the top.

Bake for 20 minutes. Increase the oven temperature to 400°F and bake for an additional 10 minutes, or until golden brown and bubbly. Allow to stand at room temperature for 10 minutes before serving.

Note

This recipe gives well. Just assemble the pie, top with mashed potatoes and cheese, and omit the puff pastry. Deliver with instructions to bake at 375°F for 30 minutes, or until the potatoes and cheese are beginning to brown. Feel free to substitute instant mashed potatoes for the real deal if you need a shortcut.

COMFORT CHICKEN POT PIE

I call it a compassion meal. It's the meal you take to your neighbor when you hear she lost her mama. It's the meal you take to a young couple whose toddler is terribly ill. It's the meal you pack up and take to a couple who is heartbroken by infertility. It's the meal Julia Robinson brought to Sam and me in 1998 when I was on bed rest with my pregnancy and Sam had just endured his second knee surgery after an injury. A compassion meal. It's a meal that you've poured your heart into on behalf of someone who needs to feel loved on, cared for, supported. Compassion meals travel well, reheat easily, and can be sent in a throw-away pan. There's a list of my favorite recipes for this very purpose in the Recipes that Give chapter (page 221). But this chicken pot pie is at the top of my list. Love Welcome Serve, y'all.

2 large boneless, skinless chicken breasts

Salt

1 tablespoon + 2 tablespoons unsalted butter

1 cup chicken stock

1 cup heavy cream, plus more for brushing

Olive oil

1½ cups sliced carrots

1 medium onion, chopped

2 garlic cloves, chopped

2 cups frozen green beans

1 cup frozen peas

¼ cup all-purpose flour

1 (14.5-ounce) can whole new potatoes, drained and quartered

1 teaspoon minced fresh thyme (optional)

Ground black pepper

¼ cup grated Parmesan cheese

1 pie dough round, purchased or homemade (page 180)

Set the oven to 400°F.

Place the chicken breasts in a single layer in a saucepan and pour in enough water to just cover them. Season the water with several heavy pinches of salt. Bring the water just to a boil, then cover with a lid and reduce to a low simmer. Allow the chicken to simmer on low for about 30 minutes. When the chicken is done, it should shred easily with two forks. After shredding, set aside.

In a small saucepan, melt 1 tablespoon butter over low heat. Add the chicken stock and cream and allow to just get warm.

In a large saucepan, heat a bit of olive oil over medium heat. Add the carrots and onion and sauté until just starting to soften. Add the garlic and stir until fragrant. Stir in the frozen green beans and peas. Shake the flour over all the vegetables and stir to coat. Slowly stir in the warm stock-cream mixture, reduce the heat to low, and allow the mixture to simmer a little. Stir in the new potatoes, thyme (if using), and shredded chicken. Season generously with salt and pepper; taste and adjust. The sauce should taste well salted.

Spoon the mixture into a deep pie dish. Cut the remaining 2 tablespoons butter into little bits and scatter them over the top. Grate on some Parmesan, then place the pie crust on top. Crimp the edges and cut several slits on top to allow the steam to vent. Brush the crust with a little cream so it will bake up golden brown. Sprinkle the crust with salt and pepper. Bake for 20 to 25 minutes, or until the crust is golden brown and the mixture is thick and bubbling.

CREAMY BACON SPINACH RAVIOLI

There's an Italian restaurant in Fayetteville, Arkansas, that we love so much it has become our default date night choice. Their bacon spinach ravioli makes my heart sing. I was determined to learn how to make a version of it at home. And gang, I've done a pretty good job if ya ask me. I've made it for lots of people, and everyone is crazy about it! It's the kind of dish that makes you sad when you take your last bite because you don't want it to be over. It's so rich and creamy that you may have to go lie down on the couch after dinner, but you'll have no regrets.

6 slices bacon, chopped

2 shallots, sliced

1 garlic clove, chopped

4 tablespoons (½ stick) unsalted butter

1 cup heavy cream

¼ cup chicken stock

1 cup grated Parmesan cheese, plus more for serving

Salt

Ground black pepper

1 (16- to 18-ounce) package refrigerated cheese ravioli (or filling of your choice)

6 ounces baby spinach leaves (about 4 cups)

1 cup halved cherry or grape tomatoes

2 tablespoon chopped fresh basil

Red pepper flakes (optional)

Bring a large pot of well-salted water to a boil over high heat so it'll be ready to go when it's time to boil the ravioli.

In a deep saucepan or braiser, sauté the bacon over medium heat until crisp. Transfer to a paper towel–lined plate, reserving the fat in the pan. Add the sliced shallots and sauté over low heat until tender. Stir in the garlic and sauté until fragrant. Add the butter and stir until melted. Whisk in the cream and stock. Bring to a low simmer, then stir in the Parmesan until melted. Taste for seasoning and add salt and pepper as needed.

Add the ravioli to the boiling water and cook according to the package instructions—be mindful not to overcook or the filling will seep out! In the few minutes that the ravioli is cooking, stir the spinach into the cream sauce and cover the pan to allow the spinach to wilt. Using a slotted spoon or pasta strainer, carefully transfer the cooked ravioli to the cream mixture. Fold the ravioli carefully into the sauce.

Spoon into warmed shallow dishes and top with the crumbled bacon, halved tomatoes, basil, and additional Parmesan cheese. We love a shake of red pepper flakes right over the top, too!

30-MINUTE SPINACH-ARTICHOKE PENNE

There are a lot of recipes in this book that start from scratch; this, however, is not one of them. And for good reason: T-I-M-E. Of course we need to learn how to make homemade dishes. But we also need a small arsenal of weeknight, fast-on-your-feet, lightning-quick recipes that we can make after church, before our Tuesday night meeting, and whenever we open our door to last-minute company. This recipe is surprisingly simple, and loaded with flavor. I think it's sure to become a favorite of yours!

1 pound penne pasta

2 tablespoons unsalted butter

2 tablespoons olive oil

1 small yellow onion, chopped

2 garlic cloves, minced

1 (14-ounce) can artichokes, drained and roughly chopped

6 ounces baby spinach leaves (about 4 cups)

2 (15-ounce) jars Alfredo sauce

1 teaspoon Creole seasoning

½ cup shredded Parmesan cheese, plus more for sprinkling

1 whole rotisserie chicken, meat shredded with two forks, skin and bones discarded

2 tablespoons drained capers (optional)

Grated zest of 1 lemon

1 cup halved grape or cherry tomatoes

Bring a large pot of well-salted water to a boil over high heat. Add the penne and cook until al dente. Drain.

While the pasta is cooking, heat the butter and olive oil in a large sauté pan over medium-low heat. Add the onion and sauté for a few minutes, until translucent and tender. Add the garlic and artichokes and sauté, making sure the garlic doesn't burn. Add the spinach and stir until it wilts down—you may need to add it in two batches to make room. It will wilt down by more than half. Stir the onion, garlic, artichokes, and spinach together well.

Pour in the Alfredo sauce. Add a little of the hot pasta water to each jar, and shake with the lid on to loosen the rest of the good sauce inside the jar; pour into the pan. Stir the sauce and spinach mixture together until combined. Season with the Creole seasoning. Bring to a low simmer and add the Parmesan cheese, stirring until the Parmesan has melted and the sauce has come together. Taste and adjust. Reduce the heat to low and cover.

Transfer the drained pasta to your biggest serving bowl, then pour the cream sauce over it and toss to combine. Stir in the chicken and capers (if using). Add the lemon zest and stir once more. Serve in shallow pasta bowls, topped with another sprinkle of Parmesan cheese and fresh grape tomatoes.

30A PULLED PORK GRILLED CHEESE WITH VIDALIA ONIONS, GRUYÈRE, AND APPLE MUSTARD

I can distinctly remember eating my first pulled pork grilled cheese sandwich at the food trucks in Seaside, Florida, along Scenic Highway 30A. My Gracie Girl and I had decided to tool around the shops that morning to work up an appetite for lunch. We agreed on the grilled cheese truck, and this recipe is my version of the sandwich I ate that day: rich, smoky pulled pork with sweet caramelized onions and loads of melted Gruyère cheese on saucy, buttery grilled bread. So simple but with so many flavors! We people-watched and ate our grilled cheeses and made a lasting food memory! I love recreating those memories in my own kitchen.

Canola oil

2 medium Vidalia onions, sliced

¼ cup apple jelly

2 teaspoons Dijon mustard

3 to 4 cups leftover Braised Pulled Pork (page 68) or Sam's Smoked Pulled Pork (page 63)

8 slices hearty bread, like farmhouse style

2 cups shredded Gruyère cheese

Unsalted butter, for grilling the sandwiches

Swirl a skillet with a little canola oil, then sauté the onions over medium heat, stirring occasionally, until tender and caramelized, about 20 minutes.

While the onions cook, in a small bowl, stir together the apple jelly and Dijon mustard; set aside. Heat up the pulled pork in a covered saucepan over low heat.

Preheat a skillet with a lid over medium heat. Build each sandwich by spreading a slice of bread with apple mustard, then piling on the pulled pork, onions, and Gruyère cheese. Top each with a second slice of bread. Melt a tablespoon of butter in the hot skillet, add the sandwich, and cover the skillet with the lid to allow the heat to melt the cheese and warm the inside of the sandwich. Remove the lid, pick up the sandwich, add another tablespoon of butter, and grill the other side of the sandwich without the lid. Remove the sandwich when the bread is golden brown and the cheese is melted. Repeat with the remaining sandwiches (you can do two or more at a time if your skillet is large enough; just add extra butter). Serve with more apple mustard on the side for dipping, if you like.

BAKED SOUTHERN REUBEN SANDWICHES WITH HOMEMADE THOUSAND ISLAND

I have vivid memories of my mama making Reuben sandwiches on Saturday afternoons when I was growing up. I remember the smells. I remember the exact sheet pan she used (I feel sure she still has it, 30 years later!). And I remember waiting with my nose pressed up to the window in the oven door watching the cheese melt. Now that I have a kitchen and a family of my own, I've taken that memory and made the recipe my own with the addition of bacon and with chow-chow in place of the sauerkraut. This is a warm, toasty comfort sandwich everyone is sure to love!

6 to 8 slices bacon, cut in half

½ cup mayonnaise

1 tablespoon ketchup

1 tablespoon chili sauce

2 teaspoons sweet pickle relish

1 teaspoon white vinegar

1 teaspoon sugar

1 tablespoon minced shallot

Red pepper flakes

Unsalted butter, at room temperature, for spreading

8 slices good marble rye or pumpernickel bread

8 slices aged Swiss cheese

1½ pounds good-quality deli corned beef, thinly sliced

2 cups Pickled Chow-Chow (page 50), liquid squeezed out

Set the oven to 425°F.

In a skillet, sauté the bacon over medium heat until crisp. Transfer to a paper towel–lined plate.

In a small bowl, make the Thousand Island dressing by whisking together the mayonnaise, ketchup, chili sauce, relish, vinegar, sugar, shallot, and a shake of red pepper flakes. Set aside.

Generously butter one side of each slice of bread. Lay four slices of bread, buttered side down, on a sheet pan lined with aluminum foil. Sauce the bread with some Thousand Island dressing, then layer with a piece of cheese. Pile on the corned beef, chow-chow, and a few half-slices of bacon before topping with another piece of cheese. Sauce the top piece of bread on the non-buttered side with Thousand Island and top off the sandwiches, buttered side up. Place another sheet pan on top of the sandwiches to add a little weight and hold the sandwiches together. Bake the sandwiches for 6 to 8 minutes, then remove the top sheet pan, flip the sandwiches over, and bake for another 6 to 8 minutes, or until they're toasted and the cheese is melted.

Slice on the diagonal and serve immediately.

CREAM CHEESE CHICKEN ENCHILADAS

You know that Bible verse that says, "To every thing, there is a season"? Well, for every season, there is a pan of chicken enchiladas. Yes, this recipe is at the tippy-top of my list of go-to recipes that I make for every reason in every season. I mean it: small group, company comin', the Big Game, snow day, new baby, and holiday eve. These chicken enchiladas are creamy and filling, with a little heat from jalapeño juice and a little peppery sweetness from green chiles. They can make ahead. They can freeze. They can wrap up and take easily, making them a perfect care meal. And I might even venture to say they're even better reheated on day two. There's good reason this is the most popular recipe on my blog and on Pinterest!

3 boneless, skinless chicken breasts
½ teaspoon salt, plus more for
  seasoning
1 tablespoon unsalted butter
1 teaspoon vegetable oil
1 medium yellow onion, chopped
2 (4.5-ounce) cans chopped
  green chiles
1 (8-ounce) package cream cheese
2 teaspoons ground cumin
3 tablespoons juice from jarred
  jalapeños
1½ cups + ½ cup shredded
  cheddar cheese
1½ cups + ½ cup shredded
  Monterey Jack cheese
10 large flour tortillas
2 cups heavy cream
Paprika
Chili powder
Optional toppings: chopped
  fresh cilantro, salsa, sour
  cream, and sliced avocado

Place the chicken breasts in a single layer in a saucepan and pour in enough water to just cover them. Season the water with several heavy pinches of salt. Bring the water just to a boil, then cover with a lid and reduce to a low simmer. Allow the chicken to simmer on low for about 30 minutes. When the chicken is done, it should shred easily with two forks. After shredding, set aside.

Set the oven to 350°F. Grease a 9 x 13-inch baking dish.

In a large skillet or deep saucepan, heat the butter and oil over medium heat. Add the onion and sauté until translucent. Add the green chiles with their juice and sauté for a minute or two. Turn the heat down to medium-low; add the cream cheese and stir until melted. Stir in the shredded chicken. Add the cumin, ½ teaspoon salt, and jalapeño juice. Stir well; taste for salt and add more if needed.

Pour the mixture into a large bowl. Allow it to cool for a few minutes, then add 1½ cups of each cheese, reserving ½ cup of each for later. Stir well to combine.

Spread each tortilla with the chicken-cheese mixture, roll up, and line them up in the prepared baking dish. You will need to cram them in to fit them all! If you have extra filling left after making all the enchiladas, just spread it right over the top of the rolled enchiladas. Then pour the heavy cream over the enchiladas, sprinkle the remaining ½ cup of each cheese over them, and shake a little paprika and chili powder over the top.

Cover the baking dish with aluminum foil and bake for 30 minutes. Remove the foil and bake for another 20 minutes. Turn up the heat to 375°F and bake for another 10 minutes or so, until bubbly and beginning to brown on top. Let stand for 10 minutes before serving with your favorite toppings.

EASY MOZZARELLA AND MEATBALL BAKE WITH GRILLED ITALIAN BREAD

I've gotten stopped in the grocery store on more than one occasion by people who have told me that this recipe has become a staple in their weeknight cooking repertoire! This easy mozzarella and meatball bake is quick, requires very little hands-on time, and is a comforting crowd-pleaser. Frozen meatballs, jarred red sauce, and fresh mozzarella make this dish so simple to fix for your people on any given day and for any given occasion! I like to serve the meatballs alone, on top of a bowl of pasta, or with grilled garlicky Italian bread. A little elbow grease plus a few shortcuts yields a *lot* of flavor.

¼ **cup olive oil, plus more for sautéing**
1 **(28-ounce) package frozen meatballs**
1 **yellow onion, chopped**
4 **garlic cloves, 2 chopped and 2 lightly smashed**
2 **(24-ounce) jars favorite red sauce**
1 **teaspoon sugar**
1 **teaspoon red pepper flakes**
6 **to 8 slices fresh mozzarella cheese**
1 **loaf Italian bread**
Salt
Ground black pepper
3 **or 4 fresh basil leaves, cut into a chiffonade (see Note on page 53)**

Set the oven to 375°F.

Preheat a large oven-safe skillet over medium heat. Drizzle with a bit of olive oil and sauté the frozen meatballs to get a good, brown sear. They will not be cooked through; the goal is to get color and flavor on the outside! Transfer the meatballs to a plate and set aside.

Drizzle a little more oil in the skillet and sauté the onion and chopped garlic until tender. Stir in the red sauce, sugar, and red pepper flakes. Simmer for about 5 minutes. Carefully stir the meatballs back into the sauce. Lay the mozzarella slices all over the top and bake for 20 to 25 minutes, or until the meatballs are tender and cooked through.

Meanwhile, heat ¼ cup olive oil over low heat and allow the smashed garlic cloves to float around and flavor the warming olive oil. Cut the Italian bread in half lengthwise, brush the garlicky olive oil all over the cut sides of the bread, and season with salt and pepper. Toast the bread in the oven alongside the meatballs as they finish (or grill in a preheated grill pan).

Sprinkle the basil over the meatballs when they come out of the oven. Spoon the meatballs into shallow bowls, with a hearty slice of garlic bread on the side. Eat with a spoon, fork, and knife—or whatever works!

ROAST BEEF COBBLER

This recipe is a comfort meal showstopper—and it's about as hearty as anything that comes out of my kitchen. I take tender, shredded pot roast, combine it with chunky, seared vegetables in a savory sauce, then top it all off with buttermilk biscuits. There are a lot of steps, but none are too hard, and those gathered around your table will thank you for every bit of work that went into this cozy, memorable dish. Full bellies, full hearts.

FOR THE POT ROAST

Salt

Ground black pepper

1 (2-pound) chuck roast

Vegetable oil, for the pan

1 (32-ounce) carton beef stock

1 teaspoon Worcestershire sauce

2 yellow onions, quartered

1 head garlic, unpeeled, cut in half crosswise

4 or 5 fresh thyme sprigs

FOR THE COBBLER

Vegetable oil, for the pan

3 carrots, cut into ½-inch slices

12 ounces Baby Dutch Yellow potatoes, quartered

1 teaspoon salt, plus more for seasoning

8 ounces baby portobello (cremini) mushrooms, cut in half

2 small yellow onions, quartered

12 frozen buttermilk biscuits

2 tablespoons unsalted butter

2 tablespoons + ¼ cup all-purpose flour

1 teaspoon ground black pepper

¼ cup half-and-half

Set the oven to 300°F.

Generously salt and pepper all sides of the chuck roast. Swirl the bottom of a large Dutch oven with oil and heat over high heat. Add the roast and sear all sides to get a dark crust. Pour in the beef stock, add the Worcestershire, and tuck in the onions, garlic, and thyme around the sides of the roast. Cover and cook for 4 hours, or until the beef shreds easily with two forks. Measure out 3½ cups of the beef cooking liquid. Cover and set aside the shredded roast and the cooking liquid.

For the cobbler, swirl a 12-inch cast iron skillet, braiser, or other large oven-safe pan with oil. Add the carrots and sauté over medium-high heat for 8 to 10 minutes. They should get a little brown and become tender but still remain firm on the inside. Transfer the carrots to a large bowl. Swirl the pan with more oil, add the potatoes, season well with salt, and sauté for 8 to 10 minutes, or until they become tender but still firm on the inside. Transfer to the bowl with the carrots. Swirl the pan again with oil, add the mushrooms and onions, season well with salt, and sauté for 8 to 10 minutes, or until the onions are tender and the mushrooms have softened. Transfer to the bowl with the other vegetables. Cover and set aside.

Turn the oven temperature up to 375°F. Place the biscuits on a sheet pan and parbake for 15 minutes. The bottoms of the biscuits should have just started to crisp, but the tops will still look undone. Remove the sheet pan from the oven. Turn the oven temperature down to 350°F.

In the same pan you used for the vegetables, melt the butter over medium-low heat. Using a fork, stir in 2 tablespoons flour to make a paste. Whisk in 2 cups of the reserved beef cooking liquid.

Add 1 teaspoon each of salt and pepper. Return the vegetables to the pan, then stir in about 5 cups of the shredded roast. Add another 1½ cups of beef cooking liquid to the pan to cover the meat and vegetables, leaving about 1 inch from the top of the pan. In a small bowl, whisk together the half-and-half and remaining ¼ cup flour to make a slurry; stir this into the pan. Carefully stir and simmer over low heat for 5 minutes. Taste and adjust for seasoning. Gently smooth out the roast and vegetables, pressing down into the liquid. Cover the top of the pan with the parbaked biscuits. The pan will be very full, but the filling will thicken and cook down in the oven. Bake for 23 to 25 minutes, or until the biscuits have browned and the liquid is bubbly.

Note

I use a Dutch oven for my roast, but you may also sear the meat well to get a crust, then transfer to a slow cooker for 8 hours on low with the stock, onions, garlic, and thyme.

The roast, stock, and sautéed vegetables can be made early in the day or even the day before, then covered and refrigerated.

If you feel like going the extra mile, you can skip the freezer biscuit shortcut and make homemade buttermilk biscuits. But there are a lot of steps in this recipe, so freezer biscuits are a good choice. (Note that refrigerated biscuits from a tube are not recommended for this recipe.)

LAYERED SPAGHETTI PIE

If you're like me, you've made spaghetti so often that it's in danger of getting put on the banished list. But I sure love it, so I set out to save spaghetti by giving it a makeover! I took everyone's best-loved spaghetti recipe and brought it to an entirely new level with this spaghetti pie: layers of saucy noodles, ricotta, mozzarella, and an easy seasoned bread crumb topping! I bake mine in a springform pan for extra magical presentation, but you can absolutely pile it all into a 9 x 13-inch baking dish!

1 tablespoon olive oil, plus more for drizzling

1 small yellow onion, chopped

1½ pounds ground beef (80% lean)

2 (24-ounce) jars three-cheese red sauce

1 teaspoon brown sugar

1 teaspoon + 1 teaspoon granulated garlic

½ teaspoon red pepper flakes

Salt

Ground black pepper

12 ounces angel hair pasta, cooked al dente

2 cups ricotta cheese

2 cups + 2 cups shredded mozzarella cheese

2 large eggs, lightly beaten

2 teaspoons dried oregano

2 cups seasoned croutons

Set the oven to 350°F. Bring a large pot of salted water to a boil so it's ready when it's time to boil the pasta.

Swirl the olive oil in a large saucepan and sauté the onion over medium heat for 2 to 3 minutes to begin the cooking. Add the ground beef and cook until no longer pink, breaking it up as it cooks. Spoon out and discard some of the fat. Pour the red sauce into the pan, then stir in the brown sugar, 1 teaspoon granulated garlic, red pepper flakes, and a pinch each of salt and black pepper. Bring to a boil, then lower the heat to a simmer. Cook the pasta, then drain and transfer to the pan with sauce.

In a medium bowl, stir together the ricotta, 2 cups mozzarella, eggs, oregano, remaining 1 teaspoon granulated garlic, and a pinch each of salt and black pepper.

Grease a 9- or 10-inch springform pan and set it on a sheet pan. Spread one-third of the saucy spaghetti in the bottom of the pan, then spread half of the ricotta mixture on top. Repeat with half of the remaining spaghetti, the remaining ricotta, and then finally the remaining spaghetti. Top with the remaining 2 cups shredded mozzarella. Cover loosely with aluminum foil and bake for 30 minutes.

Meanwhile, pour the croutons into a large zip-top bag, press out the air, and seal. Using a rolling pin or meat mallet, crush the croutons. Remove the foil from the springform pan, cover the top of the spaghetti pie with the crushed croutons, drizzle with a little olive oil, and bake for another 10 minutes, or until the crouton topping is golden. Remove from the oven and let stand for 10 minutes before removing the sides of the springform pan.

WEEKNIGHT CHICKEN PARMESAN

Doesn't chicken Parmesan sound terribly hard to fix at home on a weeknight? Well, this simplified version is absolutely doable. And it's scrumptious! A few shortcuts reduce the prep and cooking time, like using store-bought sauce and an easy breading mixture. We love this served with a salad and bread—simple and unfussy. And the best part is that this recipe pleases every mouth in my house and gets asked for time and time again. It's sure to become a family favorite at your house, too!

Olive oil
1 medium yellow onion, chopped
2 garlic cloves, chopped
2 (24-ounce) jars four-cheese
    red sauce
1 tablespoon unsalted butter
Sugar
½ teaspoon salt, plus a pinch
½ teaspoon ground black pepper,
    plus a pinch
2 cups seasoned croutons
1 cup panko bread crumbs
2 teaspoons dried Italian
    seasoning
3 large eggs
3 boneless, skinless chicken
    breasts, halved lengthwise to
    make 6 thin cutlets
2 cups shredded mozzarella cheese
Grated Parmesan cheese, for
    serving
Chopped fresh basil, for serving

Set the oven to 375°F.

Swirl a little olive oil in a large saucepan and sauté the onion over medium heat until tender. Add the garlic and stir until fragrant. Stir in the red sauce. Add the butter and a pinch of sugar, then season with ½ teaspoon each salt and pepper. Turn the heat down to low and simmer.

Pour the croutons into a large zip-top bag, press out the air, and seal. Using a meat mallet or rolling pin, crush the croutons into a coarse crumb. Transfer the crushed croutons to a pie plate or shallow dish and add the panko, Italian seasoning, and a pinch each of salt and pepper. Stir well to combine. In another pie plate or shallow dish, lightly beat the eggs.

Preheat a nonstick skillet over medium heat. Drizzle in a bit of olive oil. Dredge each chicken cutlet first in the egg wash and then in the bread crumb mixture, and set on a plate. Brown two or three chicken cutlets at a time in the skillet for 2 to 3 minutes per side. As they are done, transfer the crisped chicken cutlets to a wire rack set over a sheet pan.

Bake for 10 minutes. Remove the sheet pan from the oven, spoon a little sauce on top of each chicken breast, pile on the mozzarella cheese, and return to the oven for another 2 minutes or so, or until the cheese is melted. To serve, spoon some red sauce in the middle of each plate, place a piece of chicken on top, and top with a sprinkling of grated Parmesan and fresh basil.

Note

If you've got the itch to make your own red sauce from scratch, just replace the jarred sauce with my simple Homemade Red Sauce recipe (page 163)—gosh, it's good!

CORNBREAD TAMALE PIE

When it comes to gathering and feeding people, Mexican food is always a winning choice! Most recipes easily double or triple, and can be stretched with crowd-pleasing sides like chips and salsa or guacamole, good beans, and spicy corn. This recipe for cornbread tamale pie is so simple to make. And because it's rich, a little goes a long way! I suggest ground beef because it's easy and accessible, but if you have leftover carnitas or pulled pork, by all means use it! Oh my word—the richness overload will thrill your soul. This recipe is also great for advance prep for those late-night sleepovers when kids want to eat a fourth meal at 11 pm. Just have the cornbread baked and the meat made ahead of time, then assemble and bake! See why Mexican food takes the prize?!

1 (8.5-ounce) box Jiffy corn muffin mix
1 large egg, lightly beaten
⅓ cup whole milk
1 (4.5-ounce) can chopped green chiles, drained
2 to 3 tablespoons chopped jarred jalapeños or ½ fresh jalapeño, seeded and chopped
1 yellow onion, chopped
1 pound ground beef (80% lean)
1 teaspoon ground cumin
1 teaspoon chili powder
½ teaspoon paprika
½ teaspoon dried oregano
1 scant teaspoon salt
1 (14-ounce) can black beans, rinsed and drained
2 (10-ounce) cans enchilada sauce
2 cups shredded Monterey Jack cheese, plus more for serving
Optional toppings: shredded lettuce, salsa, sour cream, sliced avocado, and chopped fresh cilantro

Set the oven to 400°F.

In a small bowl, combine the corn muffin mix, egg, milk, green chiles, and jalapeños. Pour the mixture into a 10-inch cast iron skillet or other oven-safe skillet and bake for 20 to 22 minutes, or until light golden.

While the cornbread is baking, in another skillet, sauté the yellow onion and ground beef over medium heat, breaking up the beef with your spoon, until the beef is no longer pink. Drain off the fat. In a small bowl, combine the cumin, chili powder, paprika, oregano, and salt. Stir this seasoning mix into the beef and onion. Set aside.

Remove the cornbread from the oven and turn the oven temperature down to 350°F. Spread the black beans over the cornbread, then pour the enchilada sauce over the beans. Layer on the seasoned ground beef, then the shredded cheese. Cover with aluminum foil and bake for 20 minutes. Uncover and bake for 5 to 10 minutes more, or until the cheese is melted and beginning to brown. Let stand for 5 minutes, then spoon onto plates or into shallow bowls and serve with your favorite toppings.

MAMA'S MEXICAN SKILLET CASSEROLE

My mother worked a part-time job. She served in the church and community doing all kinds of things. She ironed my daddy's shirts that he wore to the bank every day because she loved doing it for him. She kept house. She gardened. She ran me and my brother around town getting us from here to there. And she cooked dinner every night. We rarely, if ever, ate out at a restaurant. And as I've gotten older, I've grown to appreciate that she served our family that way! Her recipe for Mexican chicken casserole was one of our staple dinners. This version is my own take on hers. It doesn't keep well, so it's best eaten when it's just made.

Olive oil

1 small onion, chopped

1 (10-ounce) can diced tomatoes with green chiles, partially drained

1 (7-ounce) can chopped green chiles, drained

1 (8-ounce) package cream cheese

1 cup half-and-half

Salt

Ground black pepper

3 cups shredded cooked chicken or pulled pork

1 cup shredded Monterrey Jack cheese

1 cup shredded medium cheddar cheese

1 teaspoon ground cumin

½ teaspoon paprika, plus more for topping

2 cups + 2 cups crumbled tortilla chips

10 slices Velveeta

Optional toppings: salsa verde or tomatillo salsa, sliced avocado, chopped tomato, sour cream, and chopped fresh cilantro

Set the oven to 375°F.

Swirl a little olive oil in a 12-inch cast iron skillet and sauté the onion over medium heat until tender. Add the canned tomatoes and green chiles. Cook and stir for 2 minutes. Add the cream cheese and stir until melted. Add the half-and-half. Remove the pan from the heat. Season with a good pinch each of salt and pepper. Stir in the shredded chicken or pulled pork and the shredded cheeses. Season with the cumin and paprika. Add 2 cups crumbled tortilla chips and stir. Spread the mixture evenly in the skillet without mashing it down. Top with the Velveeta slices laid out to cover the top. Spread the remaining 2 cups crumbled tortilla chips all over the top, drizzle with olive oil, and sprinkle with additional paprika for color.

Bake for 20 to 25 minutes, or until the liquid is bubbling around the sides and the chips are just starting to brown. Remove from the oven and scoop onto plates. Serve with your choice of toppings.

Note

If you don't have an oven-safe skillet, just pour the mixture into a 9 x 13-inch casserole dish.

If you're using rotisserie chicken, be sure to taste as you go so the filling isn't too salty.

KITCHEN SINK FRITTATA

Frittatas are perfect for breakfast, brunch, lunch, or dinner any day of the week. And the beauty of a frittata is that you can toss just about anything into the mix! I pulled this recipe together one Saturday morning after we'd returned from a trip and had very few groceries in the house. I started rummaging around to see what was in the pantry and fridge, and the rest is history!

12 large eggs

½ cup whole milk

1 teaspoon salt

½ teaspoon ground black pepper

Freshly grated nutmeg

1 tablespoon unsalted butter

Olive oil

1 red onion, halved and thinly sliced

1 yellow onion, halved and thinly sliced

7 ounces (about half of a 15-ounce jar) roasted red peppers, drained well and chopped

1 (14.5-ounce) can whole new potatoes, drained and quartered

8 ounces good deli ham, chopped

2 cups shredded Monterey Jack cheese

Grated Parmesan or Gruyère cheese, for serving

Fresh thyme leaves, for garnish

Set the oven to 375°F.

In a large bowl, whisk together the eggs, milk, salt, pepper, and a little grated nutmeg. Set aside.

Swirl the butter and a bit of olive oil in a 10- or 11-inch oven-safe nonstick skillet and sauté the onions over medium heat until tender and starting to color. Stir in the red peppers, potatoes, and ham. Sauté for a minute or two, until just warmed. Turn the heat down to medium-low and spread the mixture loosely and evenly throughout the skillet. Cover with a layer of Monterey Jack cheese. Pour the egg mixture over the filling and cook for a minute or two, just until the edges begin to set.

Bake for 12 to 15 minutes, or until the center is just set. The middle may still jiggle just a bit like a custard. Allow to cool for 10 minutes or so, which will help set the eggs further. Carefully cut into wedges and serve from the skillet. Or carefully loosen the frittata by running a butter knife around the edges and sliding the frittata out of the pan and directly onto a cutting board. Top with grated Parmesan or Gruyère cheese, and garnish with fresh thyme leaves.

SOUTHERN BREAKFAST BOWL

My Gracie Girl's best friend Emily Kate goes to Samford University in Birmingham. Those girls have been best friends since they were four years old. Needless to say, Grace visits Emily Kate in Birmingham as often as she can! A big part of their time together in Alabama is spent eating. Grace had a grits bowl one time that she photographed, sent to me, and insisted that I try to make at home. While this grits bowl has considerably different ingredients than the one she had at that restaurant, it was certainly inspired by it! A bowl of stone-ground grits, creamy with white cheddar and cream, piled with sweet potato hash and a fried egg. It's rich, it's filling, and it's about as Southern as can be. Y'all enjoy!

FOR THE GRITS

3 cups water

2 cups whole milk

1 cup stone-ground grits

1 teaspoon salt

1½ cups shredded white cheddar cheese

4 tablespoons (½ stick) unsalted butter

¼ cup heavy cream

½ teaspoon granulated garlic

FOR THE HASH

Vegetable oil

1 large sweet potato, peeled and cut into ½-inch dice

Salt

1 large baking potato, peeled and cut into ½-inch dice

1 large yellow onion, chopped

1 bunch collards, ribs trimmed away and leaves roughly chopped

1½ cups diced country ham

Red pepper flakes

2 tablespoons unsalted butter

FOR THE EGGS

Coconut oil

4 large eggs

Salt

Ground black pepper

Red pepper flakes, for topping

Grated Parmesan cheese, for topping

Chopped fresh cilantro, for topping

In a deep saucepan, bring the water and milk to a boil over medium heat. Slowly pour in the grits, whisking continuously. Season with the salt. Return to a boil, whisking often. Boil and whisk for about 1 minute, then turn the heat down to low and simmer, whisking often, for 30 to 45 minutes. The grits should be very creamy and loose. If at any point the grits are too thick, just whisk in a few tablespoons of water to loosen. Just before serving, stir in the shredded cheese, butter, heavy cream, and garlic. Taste for salt, but do not oversalt because the hash will be savory.

While the grits are cooking, preheat a large cast iron skillet over medium heat for at least 5 minutes. Swirl the pan with just enough vegetable oil to cover the bottom. Add the sweet potatoes and spread them in a single layer, but don't stir them. Let them sit still so they'll form a good char on the bottom. Use a spatula to flip them over after a minute or so. Season with salt to taste. Stir in the baking potato and chopped onion. Use a flipping-folding motion more than a stirring motion so the potatoes don't come apart. Season again with salt. Cover with a lid and cook for a few minutes to help soften the potatoes. Remove the lid and carefully fold in the collards, ham, and a pinch of red pepper flakes, then add the butter. Reduce the heat and cover to allow the ham to heat through and the collards to wilt.

In a nonstick skillet over medium heat, melt several tablespoons of coconut oil. Crack an egg in the pan and allow it to cook until it begins to turn opaque. Carefully tip the pan and use a soup spoon to ladle the hot coconut oil onto the egg whites to help set them. Just as the whites are finished setting, spoon a few spoonfuls of coconut oil over the yolk to warm it. Salt and pepper the egg in the pan.

To serve, spoon about 1½ cups grits in the bottom of a shallow bowl and slide the egg out of the pan and onto one side of the grits in the bowl. Heap some hash onto the other side of the bowl, pour the coconut oil from the egg pan over the hash and grits, then sprinkle with red pepper flakes, grated Parmesan, and cilantro. Serve immediately. Repeat with the other three servings.

No. 5

SERVE ALONGSIDES

❦

They broke bread in their homes and ate together
with glad and sincere hearts.
—Acts 2:46 (NIV)

BACON AND BROWN SUGAR COLLARDS

My preacher husband is a soul food guy. He chooses it if we go out to dinner. He asks for it when I want to cook him a special meal. He loves the flavors, the smokiness, the earthiness. Although soul food was birthed out of slavery and those days following when folks were living on so little, I appreciate the hands and heart behind it. Making rich recipes out of scraps and leftovers. Crafting meals out of vegetables that were cultivated by hand. And I'll tell you, making the most out of what you've been given is a good way to live. Serve these collards alongside Sunday Red Beans and Rice (page 87). Mmmmm.

2 bunches collard greens
6 slices bacon, chopped
1 sweet onion, chopped
3 garlic cloves, minced
½ to 1 cup beef or chicken stock
1 teaspoon salt
2 tablespoons brown sugar
½ to 1 teaspoon red pepper flakes

Cut the green leaves away from the center ribs of the collard greens and discard the ribs. Stack several leaves on top of one another, roll them up like a cigar, and slice crosswise to make ribbons. (Alternatively, tear the leaves from the ribs and then tear them into 2-inch pieces.)

In a large sauté pan with deep sides and a lid, sauté the bacon over medium heat until crisp. Transfer to a paper towel–lined plate, reserving 3 tablespoons of the bacon fat in the pan. Add the sweet onion to the pan and sauté in the bacon fat until tender. Add the garlic and stir for about a minute, or until it becomes fragrant. Pour in ½ cup stock. Add the greens, about a third at a time, allowing them to wilt a little before adding more. When all the greens are in the pan, season with the salt and stir well, then cover and turn the heat down to medium-low. Allow the greens to cook down for about 10 minutes, stirring occasionally and adding up to ½ cup more stock if you like your collards more liquidy. Stir in the brown sugar and red pepper flakes, cover, and cook for another 10 minutes. Taste for seasoning and adjust as needed. Stir in the cooked bacon pieces just before serving.

SPICY SKILLET BBQ BEANS

We have gathered and fed neighbors, offensive linemen, summer camp counselors, church staff, family members, extended family members, Lambda Chis, Kappa Kappa Gammas, and a jillion other groups of people. Have you caught on to that yet? Well, it's true! And my hope is that this book will equip you with doable recipes that will expand your hospitality heart! We always make several pans of these skillet beans when we fix our BBQ menu. Sweet, spicy, smoky, and bacon-y—all the things that beans should be.

6 slices bacon, chopped

1 medium yellow onion, chopped

2 (28-ounce) cans pork and beans, drained

3 tablespoons chopped jarred jalapeños with juice

¼ cup dark brown sugar

½ cup barbecue sauce

1 tablespoon blackened seasoning

Liquid smoke

In a large skillet, sauté the chopped bacon over medium heat until crisp. Use a slotted spoon to transfer the bacon to a paper towel–lined plate, reserving the bacon fat in the pan. Add the onion to the pan and sauté until tender. Stir in the pork and beans, jalapeños, brown sugar, barbecue sauce, blackened seasoning, and a dash of liquid smoke. Taste and add more sugar, jalapeños or their juice, or blackened seasoning if needed. Simmer on low for about 30 minutes, or until the liquid reduces and thickens. Stir in the crispy bacon pieces just before serving.

AUNT NANCE'S JALAPEÑO CORN CASSEROLE

There isn't much that's not to love about my sister-in-law Nancy. She's smart and kind. She's warm and funny. She serves people like nobody else. She loves her husband and boys like crazy. She traveled at least 3 hours every Friday night to watch my Luke play football during his senior season. She is loyal, thoughtful, easygoing, and just plain fun. And she makes this corn casserole, y'all. It's old-fashioned like a dish you'd take to a church potluck. Tried, true, and people-pleasing. You may just lick your plate.

---

4 tablespoons (½ stick) unsalted butter

1 cup chopped celery

½ cup chopped yellow onion

8 ounces Velveeta, diced

1 (15-ounce) can whole corn, drained

2 (14.5-ounce) cans cream-style corn

1 cup cooked white rice

10 to 12 jarred jalapeño slices, chopped, plus 2 to 3 tablespoons jalapeño juice

2 tablespoons sugar

Set the oven to 350°F.

In a large saucepan, melt the butter over medium-low heat. Add the celery and onion and sauté until tender. Add the diced Velveeta, stirring constantly until melted. Add all the corn, the cooked rice, jalapeños and juice, and sugar. Stir well. Pour the mixture into a 9 x 13-inch baking dish or oval casserole and bake for 30 minutes.

Note

The corn casserole can be prepared and poured into the casserole dish the day before it needs to be baked and served. And reheated leftovers are the best!

ROASTED SWEET POTATOES
WITH RED PEPPER HONEY

I traveled with my preacher husband to Oklahoma City last year for a conference where he was a keynote speaker for thousands of college students. I fully expected to be changed that weekend, but I had no idea that it would be sweet potatoes that would change my life. Yes, sweet potatoes—specifically, the ones we ate at a café downtown called Kitchen No. 324. I just had to come home and create a copycat recipe of my own. Theirs are fabulous, but mine are pretty darn good. It's practically a worship experience if you ask me.

3 medium sweet potatoes, peeled and cut into ½-inch-thick slices
3 to 4 tablespoons olive oil
Salt
Ground black pepper
6 slices bacon, chopped
⅓ cup honey
1 teaspoon red pepper flakes
4 ounces goat cheese, crumbled
3 tablespoons chopped fresh chives

Set the oven to 425°F.

Lay the sweet potato slices in a single layer on a sheet pan. Drizzle with olive oil and a good pinch each of salt and pepper. Using your fingers, turn over each slice and then back again, making sure to get oil on both sides. Roast for 15 minutes, turn the slices over, and return to the oven for another 10 to 15 minutes, or until the slices are a little browned in spots but still fork-tender.

While the potatoes roast, sauté the chopped bacon in a skillet over medium heat until crisp; transfer to a paper towel–lined plate.

Warm the honey and red pepper flakes in a small saucepan over low heat. Allow to barely simmer.

When the potatoes are finished, remove them from the oven; season once more with a pinch of salt while they're hot. To serve, layer 4 or 5 slices on each plate, drizzle with the warm honey, and top with the crisped bacon, crumbled goat cheese, and chopped chives.

Note

When you're choosing sweet potatoes for this recipe, look for ones that are narrow and long and uniform in shape so they roast evenly and lay out pretty on a plate!

This recipe also makes a delicious appetizer: Just drizzle and garnish 2 or 3 sweet potato rounds on small plates for company! You can practically eat it with your fingers—and believe me, I know.

BAKED JALAPEÑO REFRIED BEANS

Mexican food is always a winner! These jalapeño refried beans are a delicious side to go with just about any taco, enchilada, or quesadilla that you can whip up. They also double as a spicy baked bean dip when served with warmed tortilla chips. Yum!
Taste as you go, spice it up, and use fresh jalapeños if you like!

2 (14-ounce) cans traditional refried beans
¾ cup whole sour cream
3 tablespoons jarred chopped jalapeños, plus 1 to 2 teaspoons jalapeño juice
1 teaspoon chili powder
½ teaspoon ground cumin
2 cups shredded medium cheddar cheese
Chopped fresh cilantro, for garnish

Set the oven to 375°F.

In a bowl, stir together the refried beans, sour cream, jalapeños and juice, chili powder, and cumin. Spread in an 8- to 10-inch cast iron skillet or casserole dish. Top with the shredded cheddar. Bake for 20 to 25 minutes, or until the cheese is melted and the beans look baked and browning around the sides. Garnish with fresh cilantro.

CREAMY STEAKHOUSE MUSHROOMS

Steak and mushrooms are a match made in heaven, and these mushrooms are divine—savory, rich, earthy, and creamy. They smell amazing when they're simmering away on the stove. I serve these with any kind of beef, on it or beside it. I spoon them over rice, mashed potatoes, or pasta. It's one of Sam's favorite sides!

1½ pounds portobello mushrooms
1 tablespoon unsalted butter
2 tablespoons olive oil
1 shallot, chopped
Salt
2 garlic cloves, lightly smashed
1 cup beef stock
½ cup dry sherry
1 tablespoon spicy brown mustard
1 teaspoon Worcestershire sauce
¼ cup heavy cream
Leaves from 2 or 3 fresh thyme sprigs

Wipe the mushrooms with a paper towel to remove any dirt or grit. Remove any stems that are especially tough. Cut the mushrooms into ½-inch-thick slices.

In a large saucepan or a cast iron skillet with a lid, melt the butter and oil over medium-low heat. Sauté the shallot just until fragrant. Add the mushrooms to the pan, sprinkle with salt, cover with the lid, and increase the temperature to medium. Allow to cook for 10 minutes, stirring occasionally. The mushrooms will cook down and turn a pretty brown. Remove the lid and drop the smashed cloves of garlic into the pan, then stir in the stock, sherry, mustard, and Worcestershire. Simmer, uncovered, for 10 minutes, stirring occasionally. Add the cream and the fresh thyme and simmer, uncovered, for another 10 to 20 minutes, or until reduced and thickened. Taste for salt and adjust as needed.

GRUYÈRE MASHED POTATOES

Mashed potatoes round out so many main course meals. We serve these alongside pork chops, steaks, tenderloin, chicken, and just about any other kind of meat. The Gruyère is a nice, nutty alternative to regular Parmesan or white cheddar, but those will certainly work if they're what you have on hand. If you've got any little bit of pan drippings left from a main course meat, by all means, make a gravy for these potatoes. It's the decent thing to do.

1¾ pounds petite Yukon Gold potatoes, quartered
1 teaspoon salt, plus more for seasoning
½ cup heavy cream
½ cup chicken stock
4 tablespoons (½ stick) unsalted butter
1 garlic clove, chopped
1 cup grated Gruyère cheese
¼ cup chopped fresh chives
Ground black pepper

Put the potatoes in a large pot and cover them with cold water by about 2 inches. Add 1 teaspoon salt. Cover the pot and bring to a boil over medium-high heat, then reduce to a simmer and cook the potatoes for 15 to 20 minutes, or until fork-tender and the skin is starting to come loose.

While the potatoes are boiling, combine the cream, stock, butter, and chopped garlic in a small saucepan; warm over low heat. Drain the potatoes, return to the pot, and pour in the warmed cream mixture. Carefully mash with a potato masher, stirring and mashing until partly chunky and partly creamy. Stir in the grated cheese and chives. Salt and pepper well to taste.

EUNA MAE'S MACARONI AND CHEESE

I can remember pulling up a stool and watching my grandmother Euna Mae cook family suppers in her kitchen. And as with every cook, a few recipes become signature dishes. Recipes that people ask for time and time again. Recipes that people think about and long for. This macaroni and cheese is one of her signatures, and it has now become one of mine. There is not one fancy thing about it. But what sets it apart is the time it spends in the oven getting a little bit dried out on top while still being undeniably gooey and creamy inside. The large elbow noodles serve as perfect jumbo carriers for all the melted cheese, so every bite is a rich, squishy dream. It fills many, travels well, and makes hearts happy.

1½ pounds large elbow noodles
16 tablespoons (2 sticks) unsalted butter
2 pounds Velveeta
1 to 1¾ cups half-and-half
Salt
Ground black pepper

Set the oven to 300°F. Lightly grease a 9 x 13-inch baking dish.

Bring a large pot of well-salted water to a boil over high heat. Boil the elbow noodles until al dente, just a minute or so less than the package suggests. While the noodles are boiling, cut the butter into 1-tablespoon pats and cut the Velveeta into 1-inch cubes.

Drain the pasta and pour it into the prepared baking dish. Add the butter pats and cheese cubes to the noodles, tucking the pieces underneath and all around evenly throughout the dish. Slowly and evenly pour over 1 cup half-and-half. Cover with aluminum foil and bake for 20 minutes, then uncover and stir. Continue to bake, uncovered, for 10 minutes and stir again. Repeat one or two more times, until the butter and cheese are melted and gooey. Add up to ¾ cup additional half-and-half to get the consistency you like. Season with salt and pepper to taste.

Increase the oven temperature to 375°F and cook for a final 5 to 7 minutes, or until the very edges of the noodles dry out and get the teeniest bit golden. Serve hot out of the oven.

ROASTED HONEY-BALSAMIC BRUSSELS SPROUTS

We love Brussels sprouts every which way—whether shaved in a salad or sautéed in a saucepan. But I have to say that these roasted Brussels sprouts are our favorite. I even introduced them for the first time into our traditional holiday menu that hadn't seen a change in decades, and they were welcomed with open arms—and open mouths! The flavor of the caramelized, roasted spots on the sprouts plus the tangy, sweet honey-balsamic glaze is magic. This is surely the way God intended Brussels to be eaten when He thought them up.

2 pounds Brussels sprouts, trimmed and halved

4 to 6 slices bacon, chopped

5 garlic cloves, quartered

Olive oil

Juice of 1 lemon

Salt

Ground black pepper

¼ cup balsamic vinegar

¼ cup honey

Leaves from 2 fresh rosemary sprigs

½ teaspoon red pepper flakes

Set the oven to 425°F.

Put the sprouts, bacon pieces, and garlic on a large sheet pan. Drizzle well with olive oil and lemon juice. Sprinkle with a good dose of salt and pepper. Rub the sprouts around with your hands to coat them well, then spread them out in a single layer. Bake for 30 minutes, tossing the sprouts halfway through.

Meanwhile, in a small saucepan, stir together the balsamic and honey over medium heat. Bring just to a boil, then turn the heat down to a simmer, allowing the mixture to reduce for about 5 minutes.

Transfer the Brussels to a pretty serving bowl. Stir the rosemary and red pepper flakes into the glaze, then pour it over the Brussels, stirring to combine.

CREAMY SOUTHERN STONE-GROUND GRITS

When I visited Savannah, I had a life-changing conversation with my cab driver. I was gushing with pride about living in the South, and she straight-out told me that Arkansas shouldn't be considered a Southern state because we serve potatoes more than we serve grits. She declared that real Southerners serve grits. Well, that was that. I was determined to start a grits way of life in Arkansas like a true Southerner. There's a way to make good stone-ground grits: low and slow, with a 5:1 ratio of liquid to grain. This recipe has white cheddar stirred in, but you could easily use sharp cheddar or even Parmesan or Gruyère.

3 cups water

2 cups whole milk

1 cup stone-ground grits

1 teaspoon salt

1½ cups shredded white cheddar cheese

4 tablespoons (½ stick) unsalted butter

¼ cup heavy cream

½ teaspoon granulated garlic

In a deep saucepan, bring the water and milk to a boil over medium heat. Slowly pour in the grits, whisking continuously. Season with salt. Return to a boil, whisking often. Boil and whisk for about 1 minute, then turn the heat down to low and allow to simmer for 30 to 45 minutes, whisking often. The grits should be very creamy and loose. If at any point the grits are too thick, just whisk in a few tablespoons of water to loosen. Just before serving, stir in the shredded cheese, butter, heavy cream, and garlic. Taste for salt and adjust.

CHEESY GARLIC POTATO GRATIN

These potatoes are worth every bit of work, every slice of the knife, every swipe of the grater, and every measured ingredient. Starchy layers of thin potatoes and Parmesan cheese swim in a garlicky cream sauce that is topped off with more cheese and a buttery crumb. This gratin can be prepared, layered, and sauced in advance, just waiting to be crumbed and baked. It's a shameful splurge, but I think you'll agree that it's worth it.

2 pounds baking potatoes, peeled

2 cups heavy cream

2 tablespoons unsalted butter

3 garlic cloves, chopped

3 tablespoons minced shallot

¼ teaspoon cayenne pepper

1 teaspoon salt, plus more for seasoning

½ teaspoon ground black pepper

1 cup grated Parmesan cheese

1½ cups shredded white cheddar cheese

1 cup seasoned bread crumbs

Olive oil

Chopped fresh chives, for garnish (optional)

Set the oven to 375°F. Lightly grease a 9 x 13-inch baking dish or casserole.

Using a good knife or mandoline, carefully slice the potatoes as thinly as possible; set aside.

In a small saucepan, combine the heavy cream, butter, garlic, shallot, and cayenne. Warm over medium-low heat just enough to melt the butter. Season with 1 teaspoon salt and the black pepper. Remove the pan from the heat.

In the prepared baking dish, layer one-third of the potatoes, give them a light sprinkle of salt, then scatter on half of the Parmesan cheese. Repeat with half of the remaining potatoes, another sprinkle of salt, and the remaining Parmesan cheese. Finish off with the remaining potatoes and a sprinkle of salt. Carefully pour the cream mixture over the layers of potatoes and cheese. Top with the shredded white cheddar cheese.

Cover the dish with aluminum foil or a lid and bake for 40 minutes. Remove the foil or lid, cover with the bread crumbs and a drizzle olive oil. Bake, uncovered, for another 10 minutes, or until the potatoes are tender and the bread crumbs are toasted. Let stand for 10 minutes before garnishing with chopped chives (if using).

SWEET POTATO SOUFFLÉ
WITH BUTTERY PRALINE TOPPING

You know the feeling when you've eaten so much that you nearly pop? Then you moan and groan about how you shouldn't take one more bite? This sweet potato soufflé is my sister-in-law Lori's specialty, and it's the bite that I cannot leave on my plate no matter how stuffed I am. It would be a sin. With all its buttery, brown sugary, nutty goodness, it's practically dessert. And did I mention that it makes an enormous vat? It does, making it ideal for serving a crowd if you've got one to feed.

FOR THE SOUFFLÉ
- **6 medium sweet potatoes, peeled and diced**
- **8 tablespoons (1 stick) unsalted butter**
- **4 large eggs, lightly beaten**
- **2 teaspoons vanilla extract**
- **1 cup white sugar**
- **1 teaspoon salt**
- **½ teaspoon ground cinnamon**

FOR THE TOPPING
- **8 tablespoons (1 stick) unsalted butter, at room temperature**
- **1½ cups brown sugar**
- **6 tablespoons all-purpose flour**
- **1 cup pecan chips**

Set the oven to 325°F. Lightly grease the bottom and sides of the largest, deepest 9 x 13-inch baking dish or casserole that you have.

Bring a large pot of water to a boil over medium-high heat. Boil the sweet potatoes for 15 minutes, or until tender. Drain the potatoes and return them to the pot, add the butter, and mash it into the potatoes until they're smooth. Add the eggs, vanilla, white sugar, salt, and cinnamon and stir well to combine. The mixture will be soupy. Pour the sweet potato mixture into the prepared baking dish.

In a medium bowl, use a fork to mix the room-temperature butter, brown sugar, flour, and pecan chips. Carefully distribute the topping mixture over the sweet potatoes. Cover with aluminum foil and bake for 35 minutes. Remove the foil and continue to bake for 10 to 15 minutes more, or until the middle is set.

SWEET BUTTERMILK CORNBREAD

I have memories of my Papa Nelson eating cornbread for supper. If my memory serves me right, he ate it every Wednesday night when I was at his house while my parents went to choir practice at the Baptist church. And what cornbread he didn't eat with his beans, he would crumble up in a glass, soak in milk, and eat with a spoon like dessert. That goes to show that cornbread is good just about any way you can imagine.

4 tablespoons (½ stick) unsalted butter

1½ cup all-purpose flour

1 cup plus 2 tablespoons yellow cornmeal

3 tablespoons sugar

1 tablespoon baking powder

1 teaspoon salt

1½ cups buttermilk

2 large eggs

3 tablespoons salted butter, melted

Set the oven to 400°F. Put the unsalted butter in a 10-inch cast iron skillet and put it in the oven to melt while the oven heats.

Meanwhile, stir together the flour, cornmeal, sugar, baking powder, and salt in a medium bowl. In a separate bowl, whisk together the buttermilk and eggs. Stir the wet ingredients into the dry. The mixture will be thick.

Carefully remove the hot skillet from the oven when the butter is melted. Pour the hot butter into the cornmeal mixture; stir to combine. Spread the batter in the hot skillet and bake for 28 to 30 minutes, or until golden brown. As soon as it comes out of the oven, brush the salted butter over the entire top of the cornbread in the pan.

Note

Make sure your baking powder is fresh so you get lift in your cornbread.

Sam insists that cornbread can never been sweet enough, so feel free to adjust the sugar to make this sweeter or less sweet to suit your people.

You can divide this batter up in muffin tins or loaf pans or any other creative form you prefer; just adjust your baking time accordingly.

SCRATCH DINNER ROLLS

Learning how to make homemade dinner rolls is a badge of honor in my book. It takes time, patience, skill, and a lot of practice. But once you get it, you swell with pride—and deservedly so! I wanted terribly to join the ranks of Sam's grandmother and my sisters-in-law and their mothers who made good homemade dinner rolls. So I worked and practiced and ate a lot of warm rolls in the process! (It's a tough job, but somebody's gotta do it.) The result? This recipe! They're sweet, buttery, and mouthwatering—just ask my son Luke, who has been known to eat eleven rolls in one sitting.

1½ cups whole milk

8 tablespoons (1 stick) unsalted butter, cubed, plus additional melted butter for brushing

½ cup + 1 teaspoon sugar

½ cup very warm water

1 package active dry yeast

3 large eggs, lightly beaten

2 teaspoons salt

6 cups all-purpose flour, plus more for your work surface

Sea salt, for sprinkling

Set the oven to 200°F to create a warm place for the first rise.

Pour the milk into a small saucepan and bring to a simmer over medium-low heat. Remove the pan from the heat and stir in the butter cubes and ½ cup sugar; let cool.

Meanwhile, in a small bowl, gently whisk together the warm water, yeast, and remaining 1 teaspoon sugar until dissolved. Allow to rest for 10 minutes until it's foamy. It'll smell so good!

In the bowl of a stand mixer fitted with the dough hook, combine the cooled milk mixture, yeast mixture, eggs, salt, and 3 cups of the flour and mix on low speed until smooth. Add the remaining 3 cups flour, ½ cup at a time, and mix until a smooth ball forms. Scrape out the dough onto a generously floured work surface. It will be very sticky. Shake a little extra flour over the dough and knead for about 5 minutes, until the dough is combined and smooth and a gentle finger-poke in the top presses in but slowly springs back a little.

Now turn off the oven.

Place the dough in a large greased bowl, cover with a lightweight dish towel that is barely damp—and I mean barely—and let it rise in the warmed oven until it has doubled in bulk, 60 to 70 minutes. It will spread and fill the bowl more than it will actually rise up. After 30 or 35 minutes, you may turn the oven back on to 200°F for just a minute and then turn it off quickly to maintain a little heat in there, as it will have surely cooled by this time. Resist the urge to keep opening and closing the oven door. After the dough has doubled, remove the bowl from the oven.

Set the oven to 200°F again to create a warm place for the second rise. Line a large sheet pan with parchment paper or a silicone baking mat.

Turn out the dough onto a floured surface and punch the dough a few times with a firm fist to let the air out. Now pull off a ball about the size of an egg and gently roll it into a ball approximately 2½ inches in diameter. Place it on the lined sheet pan. Continue making dough balls, sprinkling the dough with a little flour so it's manageable and not sticky, and space them out on the sheet pan about 1½ inches apart.

Now turn off the oven.

Cover the rolls with a lightweight dish towel and place the sheet pan in the oven for a second rise. In 30 to 40 minutes, they should double in size. Remove the sheet pan and set the oven to 350°F.

Remove the towel and bake the rolls for about 20 minutes, or until golden brown. Remove the sheet pan from the oven and brush the tops of the rolls with melted butter and give them a light sprinkle of sea salt.

Note

It is critical that you use fresh yeast, not yeast that's been in the back of your pantry from when you moved into your house in 2003. Yeast loses its pizzazz after a few months, so be sure it's fresh or your rolls won't rise!

Making yeast dough depends on many factors; even the weather can affect the rise! I have had to let my rolls rise the second time for as long as an hour. They need to nearly double in size, so don't rush the rise!

JOHNSON COUNTY BISCUITS

My preacher husband grew up with a grandmother who made homemade biscuits just about every day, so biscuits are his love language. And not just any biscuit, but the kind that Mama Grace made. A little loft, crispy on the top and bottom, and tender on the inside. He's not into those giant, light-colored, fluffy biscuits. A Johnson County boy needs a bit of crunch, rich golden color, and a little crumble. So I set out over the course of our marriage to make him the biscuits of his childhood. He says he loves me a little more because of it, which thrills my Baxter County heart.

2½ cups all-purpose flour, plus more for your work surface

2 teaspoons sugar

1 tablespoon baking powder

1 teaspoon baking soda

1 teaspoon salt

9 tablespoons cold unsalted butter, cut into very small bits

1 cup cold buttermilk

2 tablespoons salted butter, melted

Note

These biscuits may be frozen and baked a few at a time! Prepare the recipe, forming the biscuits into their squares, then freeze them on a sheet pan. Transfer the frozen biscuits to a zip-top freezer bag. Then just bake however many you need! Add 2 to 3 minutes to the bake time when baking from frozen.

Set the oven to 400°F. Line a sheet pan with parchment or use a nonstick/easy-release pan.

In a large, wide bowl, whisk together the flour, sugar, baking powder, baking soda, and salt. With a pastry blender or two forks, cut the chilled unsalted butter bits into the dry ingredients until the mixture resembles coarse meal. Pour the cold buttermilk all around the bowl. Carefully use a wooden spoon to gently fold and stir the buttermilk until large, wet, sticky clumps form. With well-floured hands, work the mixture together in the bowl until it somewhat holds together.

Turn out the dough onto a floured surface. With well-floured hands, knead the dough about 10 times, or until it comes together, shaking a little extra flour on the dough to keep it from being too sticky. Scrape away and discard the little crumbly bits that will not incorporate into the dough. Gently pat out the dough into a rectangle that is about ¾ inch thick. Forming the dough into a rectangle (rather than using a round cutter) means that you'll be handling the dough less—and also that you'll use every bit of the dough without any scraps left! Use a large kitchen knife to cut the dough into 12 square biscuits. Cut straight down and avoid sawing back and forth, which will discourage a good rise.

Transfer the biscuits to the prepared sheet pan, placing them about 1 inch apart. Bake for 13 to 15 minutes, or until they are golden brown. Remove from the oven and brush the tops of the hot biscuits with salted butter.

No. 6

Sweet Tea, Sauces, and Such

People who love to eat are always the best people.
—Julia Child

SUNDAY SWEET TEA

On most Sunday nights for nearly 20 years, my husband and I have hosted a small group in our home. We fellowship and visit and hug and pray and connect with each other, and it always happens over food. So almost every Sunday, I make two gallons of sweet tea to serve alongside whatever food shows up in casseroles or Crock-Pots. Two gallons of sweet tea every week for almost 20 years is a lot of tea-makin' experience, so you can take my word for it that this is a recipe you can trust. And another thing you can take my word for: Good things happen over sweet tea.

6 to 8 cups water

1½ cups sugar

10 regular-size tea bags or 4 family-size tea bags

Ice

Lemon slices and/or fresh mint sprigs, for garnish (optional)

Boil the water in a teakettle or on the stovetop in a saucepan. While the water is coming to a boil, scoop the sugar into the bottom of a gallon-size pitcher. When the water comes to a boil, slowly pour it into the pitcher of sugar, stirring as you pour. Stir until the sugar is dissolved. Unwrap the tea bags and drop them down into the hot, sugary water, tags and all. Stir them into the water with a big long spoon, making sure they're submerged. Let them steep for 10 to 12 minutes. Carefully lift and remove the tea bags from the pitcher, making sure not to squeeze them, which may result in bitter tea. Stir the hot tea mixture to combine. Then fill the remaining space in the pitcher with plenty of ice. Stir and refrigerate for at least an hour before serving. Garnish with a fresh lemon slice or a sprig of mint stirred into each glass.

SWEET TEA VINAIGRETTE

We Southerners can think up all kinds of ways to use our beloved sweet tea, and this sweet, tangy vinaigrette is a perfect example. My word, it's a delicious alternative to your regular old vinaigrettes! Toss this dressing on salad greens and serve with grilled shrimp, peaches, and goat cheese, or with grilled chicken, strawberries, and feta.

½ cup Sunday Sweet Tea (page 157)
¼ cup champagne vinegar
1 teaspoon honey
1 teaspoon Dijon mustard
1 tablespoon chopped fresh chives
¾ cup fruity olive oil or canola oil
Salt

In a small bowl, whisk together the sweet tea, vinegar, honey, Dijon, and chives. Whisking continuously, slowly drizzle in the oil, then stir in a pinch of salt.

CITRUS-BASIL SWEET TEA

Sweet tea is the nectar of the South—I've made it so often I could make it in my sleep. But occasionally, it's awful fun to offer a fancier sweet tea for brunch, a girls' night, a wedding shower, or on any given afternoon. This version begins with my regular sweet tea recipe and infuses it with a simple syrup with fresh lemon and lime juices plus basil leaves. It's fresh, bright, sweet, and gooooood. I'm sipping one out of an old jam jar right this second because I practice what I preach.

---

1 cup water
1 cup sugar
Juice of 2 lemons
Juice of 3 limes
1 cup (packed) fresh basil leaves, plus more for garnish
5 cups Southern Sweet Tea (page 157)
Lime slices, for garnish

In a medium saucepan, stir the water and sugar together over medium-low heat until the sugar dissolves. Remove the pan from the heat, and stir in the lemon and lime juices (should be at least ½ cup of citrus juice). Rub the basil leaves together between your fingers to release their scent and flavor. Stir them into the sugar-citrus water. Allow to steep for at least an hour at room temperature or overnight in the refrigerator.

When time to serve, spoon out and discard the basil leaves. Pour the mixture into a pitcher, add the sweet tea, and stir to combine. Pour into glasses filled with ice and serve with lime slices and basil leaves.

Note

If you don't like basil, you may substitute mint, which is equally yummy!

For a little adult fun, feel free to splash a little sumpthin' in the glasses before pouring in the tea.

STRAWBERRIES ROMANOFF

I was 14 years old when I first had strawberries Romanoff at my Great-Great-Aunt Lorraine's house in Fullerton, California, and I do believe it was the best thing I had ever eaten. She loved to cook and host, and I remember her putting out the most beautiful breakfast spread when we stayed with her for a weekend. Sweet, creamy, and tangy, strawberries Romanoff makes a lovely breakfast, brunch, or dessert. The sauce is also delightful dolloped on pancakes, waffles, or pound cake!

½ cup cold heavy cream

3 to 4 tablespoons powdered sugar

½ cup whole sour cream

3 tablespoons brown sugar

1 tablespoon vanilla

⅛ teaspoon ground cinnamon

2 pints strawberries, hulled and halved

In the bowl of a stand mixer fitted with the whisk attachment, whip the heavy cream and powdered sugar together until it begins to thicken.

In a separate bowl, whisk together the sour cream, brown sugar, vanilla, and cinnamon. Fold the sour cream mixture into the whipped heavy cream until combined. Serve with the strawberries.

HOMEMADE RED SAUCE

There are several recipes in this book where I take a shortcut and use store-bought red sauce. But listen to me: On occasion I hope you will take a night or a Saturday afternoon and make your own homemade red sauce. It's loaded with fresh, natural ingredients, and that means flavor! You can store it in the refrigerator or even freeze it in pre-measured amounts so you can thaw exactly what you need when you need it. New family at your school or on your street? Welcome them with a jar of homemade red sauce, a package of good local pasta, and crusty bakery bread!

2 medium carrots, cut into big pieces

1 celery stalk

1 small yellow onion, quartered

4 garlic cloves, peeled

¼ cup fresh flat-leaf parsley

Olive oil

2 teaspoons salt, plus a pinch

2 (28-ounce) cans whole peeled San Marzano tomatoes

2 teaspoons sugar

2 teaspoons ground black pepper

2 tablespoons unsalted butter

2 tablespoons bacon fat

4 fresh basil leaves

Red pepper flakes

In the bowl of a food processor, pulse the carrots, celery, onion, garlic, and parsley a few times, until chopped into tiny bits but not entirely puréed. Swirl a large sauté pan with good olive oil and sauté the processed vegetables over medium-low heat for 5 to 7 minutes, until tender and cooked down. Season with a pinch of salt.

Pour the tomatoes and their juice into a large bowl and crush them with your hands. Stir the tomatoes and their juice into the pan with the sautéed vegetables. Bring to a boil, then turn the heat down to a simmer. Stir in the sugar, 2 teaspoons salt, and black pepper. Then stir in the butter and bacon fat. Finally, stir in the whole basil leaves and a pinch of red pepper flakes. Simmer for 30 to 45 minutes, stirring occasionally and making sure to scrape the sides of the pan. Taste and adjust the seasonings as the sauce simmers.

Note

The yield can vary depending on how long you allow the sauce to cook down. The longer it cooks down, the better the flavor. So let it simmer for no less than 30 minutes! You can let it go for as long as an hour if you like.

Allow to cool to room temperature before storing in the refrigerator for up to a week or in the freezer for as long as 3 months.

HOMEMADE ALFREDO SAUCE

Homemade Alfredo sauce is so simple to whip up, though I think people believe otherwise. In the time it takes to heat up jarred Alfredo, you can make your own—all natural, rich, and yummy! I assure you: Good Alfredo will bring people back to your house time and time again!

---

8 tablespoons (1 stick) unsalted butter

2 or 3 garlic cloves, lightly smashed

2 cups heavy cream

2 cups grated Parmesan cheese

Freshly grated nutmeg

Salt

Ground black pepper

In a small saucepan, melt the butter over medium-low heat. Add the garlic cloves and stir around in the warm butter for several minutes. Stir in the heavy cream and bring just to a simmer. Whisk in the grated Parmesan until melted and smooth. Simmer for 7 to 8 minutes, or until smooth and creamy. Season with a touch of grated nutmeg and a little salt and pepper. Discard the garlic cloves before serving.

Note

Allow any leftover Alfredo sauce to cool for an hour at room temperature before storing in the refrigerator for up to 4 days. Reheat, stirring to combine. You may also freeze it in quart-size freezer bags for as long as 4 months, so consider making a double batch!

COMEBACK SAUCE

There's a local chicken strip restaurant in Fayetteville called Slim Chickens that we frequent frequently. What I mean by that is we go *all the time*. As with most chicken restaurants, they have a "secret sauce" for dipping their crispy chicken fingers, French fries, fried pickles, and more. It's creamy, tangy, and a little sweet, and has a lingering heat. Here's my version of that sauce that'll keep 'em coming back for more!

1 cup mayonnaise
¼ cup chili sauce
3 tablespoons ketchup
2 tablespoons Sriracha sauce
1 teaspoon Worcestershire sauce
½ teaspoon granulated garlic
½ teaspoon onion powder
½ teaspoon dry mustard
¼ teaspoon ground black pepper
⅛ teaspoon cayenne pepper

In a small bowl, whisk together all the ingredients. Cover and refrigerate for at least 30 minutes before serving. Store in an airtight container in the refrigerator for up to 3 days.

HOMEMADE HERBY RANCH DRESSING

Ranch is America's best-selling salad dressing, overwhelmingly so over all others. So I set out to develop a homemade recipe that is fresh, contains no preservatives, and has loads of flavor. This recipe is the result! As with most dressing and sauce recipes, it's best after letting it chill for at least an hour or overnight.

1 cup mayonnaise

½ cup whole sour cream

½ cup buttermilk

1 teaspoon Dijon mustard

1 teaspoon freshly squeezed lemon juice

Worcestershire sauce

1 tablespoon minced shallot

1 garlic clove, minced

2 to 3 tablespoons minced fresh dill

1 tablespoon minced fresh flat-leaf parsley

Red pepper flakes

Salt

In a small bowl, whisk together the mayo, sour cream, buttermilk, Dijon, lemon juice, a dash of Worcestershire, shallot, garlic, dill, parsley, and a few shakes of red pepper flakes. Taste for salt and seasoning; adjust. Cover and chill for at least 30 minutes before serving.

EASY-PEASY CREAMY ITALIAN DRESSING

My people are dippers and saucers. So naturally I have an arsenal of fast, easy dressings and sauces that I whip up for quick tossed salads or for dipping bread sticks or pizza crust in. This is also one of my favorite dressings to toss on pasta salad. It's tangy, creamy, and timeless!

¾ **cup bottled zesty Italian dressing**
¼ **cup mayonnaise**
2 **tablespoons olive oil**
1 **teaspoon sugar**
1 **teaspoon dried oregano**
½ **teaspoon granulated garlic**
½ **teaspoon red pepper flakes**

In a small bowl, whisk together all the ingredients. Taste for seasonings and adjust. Cover and store in the refrigerator for up to 3 days. Whisk before serving.

HOMEMADE CHICKEN STOCK

Homemade chicken stock is one of the finer things in life. There is nothing like it in the world! Its richness is notable in your soups and sauces. The process requires little skill, but it does take some time, so you'll need to plan accordingly. Just set aside a Saturday afternoon to let the vegetables and chicken simmer away, then store it in jars in the fridge or freezer so you'll always have some handy. I like to go straight from making stock into stirring up a pot of Hearty Homemade Chicken and Dumplins (page 92). Glory!

1 (5-pound) chicken
4 medium carrots, cut in half
3 celery stalks, cut in half
2 yellow onions, quartered
4 garlic cloves
2 bay leaves
2 fresh thyme sprigs
2 fresh rosemary sprigs
1 tablespoon salt
1 tablespoon whole black
   peppercorns

Place the chicken in a 10-quart Dutch oven or stockpot. Add the vegetables (no need to peel anything!), bay leaves, thyme, rosemary, salt, and peppercorns. Fill the pot with water up to about 2 inches from the top of the pot. Bring the water just to a boil over medium heat, then turn the heat down to low. Cover the pot with the lid, leaving it slightly cracked. Simmer for at least 5 hours and as long as 7 hours, adding more hot water as the liquid cooks down, so that all the meat and veggies remain submerged. Occasionally use a fine-mesh strainer to skim the scummy foam off the top.

Using two large utensils, move the chicken to a cutting board with a juice moat. Pick off the meat and set aside to use or store for later. Then place a fine-mesh strainer over another stockpot or large bowl. Pour the stock through the strainer, allowing it to catch the vegetables and other solids. Discard the contents of the strainer.

Divide the stock among glass jars or plastic containers and allow them to cool to room temperature. Seal the containers and store in the refrigerator for up to 3 days or in the freezer for up to 3 months. Before using, spoon off and discard any fat that has formed at the top.

Note

The amount of stock you end up with depends upon how big your pot is, how much of the liquid cooks down, how much additional water you use, and so on.

CHOCOLATE SHELL TOPPING

How many times have I made this chocolate shell topping? Too many times to count! We drizzle it over our ice cream, which is always a treat. We dip bananas in it, sprinkle them with colorful nonpareils, then refrigerate them on parchment sheets for a fun snack. And we absolutely love to dip strawberries in it and refrigerate them for a little bite of something sweet. Yum!

½ cup semisweet chocolate chips
½ cup milk chocolate chips
2 tablespoons coconut oil

In a microwave-safe bowl, combine the chocolate chips and coconut oil. Microwave in 30-second intervals, stirring, until smooth.

EVERYDAY SALSA

This salsa is aptly named because we could—and do!—eat it every day. We eat it with chips, on quesadillas, on grilled chicken, beside eggs, and just about everywhere else! I love to load it with cilantro and heavy lime; my family prefers lighter cilantro and lime. Just taste and adjust until it's exactly how you like it! It's really important that you let it chill before you serve it to allow the flavors to develop.

1 (28-ounce) can whole peeled plum tomatoes, drained
2 (10-ounce) cans Ro-Tel diced tomatoes with green chiles, partially drained
1 (4-ounce) can chopped green chiles with juice
½ yellow onion, chopped
3 small garlic cloves, chopped
1 bunch fresh cilantro
Juice of 1 lime
1 teaspoon white vinegar
1 teaspoon sugar
1 teaspoon ground cumin
1 teaspoon salt

In a blender, combine all the ingredients. Blend until smooth, or pulse for a chunkier salsa. Allow to chill for at least an hour before serving. Store in an airtight jar for up to a week.

HOMEMADE SWEETENED
WHIPPED CREAM

Homemade whipped cream is easily one of the most delicious things in the world. Once I learned of the lusciousness and simplicity of homemade whipped cream, I couldn't imagine serving the kind that comes in a carton. Very cold cream is key here, so don't take it out of the refrigerator until you're ready to begin. And be sure to lick the whisk!

2 cups very cold heavy whipping cream
5 tablespoons powdered sugar
1 teaspoon vanilla extract

Place the bowl of your stand mixer and the whisk attachment in the freezer for about 15 minutes. In the cold bowl of the stand mixer fitted with the cold whisk attachment, combine the cold cream, powdered sugar, and vanilla. Whisk on high speed for about 1 minute. Do not overbeat.

SOUR CHERRY COMPOTE

A compote is a mixture of fruit that has been stewed in a sugary liquid. Sour cherries are the perfect fruit for stewing this way. In order for me to make this sour cherry compote year round, even when fresh cherries aren't in season, I use frozen tart red cherries. Don't confuse tart red cherries with black or dark red cherries, which are sweeter and better for snacking. Serve this compote warm over Lemon Ricotta Pancakes (page 199) or spoon it chilled over good vanilla ice cream.

⅔ cup water

⅔ cup sugar

1 tablespoon freshly squeezed lemon juice

1 teaspoon grated lemon zest

1 teaspoon vanilla extract

Ground cinnamon

3 cups fresh cherries, pitted, or 1 (20-ounce) bag frozen tart red cherries

In a medium saucepan, stir together the water, sugar, lemon juice, lemon zest, vanilla, and a pinch of cinnamon. Bring to a boil over medium heat and cook for about 5 minutes, or until it begins to reduce a little. Stir in the cherries and return to a boil. Cook, stirring, for another 3 to 4 minutes, or until the cherries just begin to fall apart. Mash the cherries gently, leaving some whole. Remove the pan from the heat and allow to cool completely. Store in an airtight container in the refrigerator for up to a week.

MAMA GRACE'S SAWMILL GRAVY

Sam's grandmother, Grace Ganner, was a good gal. She practically raised him and his brothers, which I imagine was quite a job. She loved pretty things like flowers, beautiful dishes, alabaster lamps, and fancy rings. But she was as tough as nails—determined and decisive, with undying devotion to her family. She taught me how to make meringue. She taught me how to cure and crack pecans. And she taught me how to make gravy. We stood over her cast iron skillet in her tiny little kitchen in the house where she raised her two girls, and she showed me how to shake the flour over the sausage and bring the heat up before turning it down to thicken. Spoon this gravy over Johnson County Biscuits (page 153).

1 pound hot ground breakfast sausage
¼ cup all-purpose flour
2 cups whole milk, or more if needed
Freshly grated nutmeg
Salt
Ground black pepper

In a 12-inch cast iron skillet, brown the sausage over medium heat, crumbling it with your spoon. Do not drain the fat. Reduce the heat to low and shake the flour over the sausage, stirring to coat well. Spread the sausage evenly across the bottom of the skillet, then pour in the milk—it should cover the top of the sausage. Grate a little fresh nutmeg into the gravy. Salt and pepper well. Raise the heat to medium and allow the sausage gravy to come just to a boil, stirring often. Turn the heat down to a simmer and allow to thicken, stirring, for just a few minutes. Taste for salt and pepper and adjust.

CLASSIC FLAKY PIE CRUST

Oh yes, I have recipes that use refrigerated pie crust, and I even have a store-bought crust in my fridge as we speak. But homemade pie crust is undeniably one of the best things ever. I don't always have the time or the want-to to make homemade crust, so when I do, I go ahead and make four. It requires the same amount of elbow grease, and it's equal the cleanup. And we know that where there's pie crust, there's pie! This crust recipe is flaky, flavorful, and just enough salty—perfect for savory and sweet pies alike!

12 tablespoons (1½ sticks) cold unsalted butter

1¾ cups cold solid vegetable shortening (such as Crisco)

1 cup ice water

2 tablespoons vodka

5¼ cups all-purpose flour

4½ teaspoons salt

Cut the cold butter and cold shortening into very small pieces on a cutting board and place the whole cutting board in the freezer. In a measuring cup, combine the ice water and vodka; place the cup in the freezer along with the butter and shortening pieces. Let all of that get very, very cold—at least 10 minutes.

In a very large mixing bowl, combine the flour and salt. Add the cold butter pieces to the flour mixture and use a pastry cutter to cut the butter into the flour until the mixture looks like coarse crumbs. Work quickly so the butter doesn't get too warm. Then add the cold shortening pieces, and continue to cut it into the flour-butter mixture. When it's cut in well, the mixture will look like clumps and curds.

Drizzle the cold water-vodka all over the dough, then use a wooden spoon to carefully incorporate the liquid without stirring it to death. The dough will not look smooth or combined like a batter would. It is ready to be turned out onto a floured surface when you can grab a little handful of it, squeeze it, and it sticks together. If the dough does not stick together, stir in additional water, a tablespoon at a time, until it's the right texture.

With two hands, gather the dough together into a slightly crumbly ball while in the bowl, then turn it out onto a lightly floured surface (a cold surface like marble or granite is better than plastic or wood). Fold the dough over onto itself just a few times, but do not overwork the dough. Gently kneading it just a few times will bring it together and smooth it a little more.

Shape the dough into a big, thick log and cut it in half and then in half again, making four equal dough sections. Place one dough section in a quart-size freezer bag. Use a rolling pin to flatten the dough to fill the bag, then seal the bag. Repeat this step for the other three dough sections. Chill the dough in the fridge for at least 30 minutes or up to 3 days.

When it's time to use a dough round, remove it from the fridge, allow it to sit out for 3 or 4 minutes, then tear down the side of the bag and turn out the dough onto a well-floured surface. Sprinkle the top generously with flour, then gently roll from the center out to make a flat round. Transfer to a pie dish or sheet pan and fill as desired.

Note

White vinegar may be used in place of vodka.

The sealed bags of pie dough may be refrigerated for up to 3 days or frozen for up to 3 months. To thaw frozen pie dough, place the bag in the refrigerator overnight.

No. 7

FOR THE LOVE OF SWEETS

Satisfy us . . . with Your unfailing love, that we may
sing for joy and be glad all our days.
—Psalm 90:14 (NIV)

GRAN'S STRAWBERRY CAKE

This cake is a classic, just like the gal who gave me the recipe. Louise Gaston was strong and kind, and spoke with a drawl as slow as honey. She was always put together. She loved her family fiercely and Jesus even more. She showed me hospitality on more than one occasion. Her loved ones called her Gran. This is her cake. It's one of my most popular recipes—made by many, and loved by all.

FOR THE CAKE

½ cup chopped fresh strawberries or frozen crushed strawberries with juice
2 to 3 tablespoons sugar
1 box white cake mix
3 tablespoons all-purpose flour
1 (3-ounce) box strawberry Jell-O (not sugar-free)
¾ cup vegetable oil
¾ cup water
3 large eggs, at room temperature
1 teaspoon vanilla extract

FOR THE STRAWBERRY GLAZE

1 cup powdered sugar
2 tablespoons unsalted butter, melted
1 teaspoon vanilla extract
¼ teaspoon almond extract

Set the oven to 350°F. Coat a Bundt pan or 9 x 13-inch baking dish with nonstick baking spray.

In a small bowl, combine the strawberries, sugar, and a splash of water. With clean hands, mash the berries into a yummy, mushy strawberry mixture. Reserve 2 tablespoons of the mushy strawberry liquid for the glaze. Set aside.

In the bowl of a stand mixer fitted with the paddle attachment, stir together the cake mix, flour, and Jell-O to combine and remove any clumps from the cake mix. With the mixer on low, pour in the oil, water, and strawberries with juice. Then add the eggs, one at a time. Add the vanilla. Increase the speed to medium-high and beat for about 2 minutes to put air in the batter. Pour into the prepared baking dish and bake for 35 to 40 minutes, or until a toothpick inserted in the middle comes out clean and moist, but not batter-y. Allow to cool for 10 to 12 minutes before inverting onto a cake plate.

While the cake is cooling, whisk together all the glaze ingredients, including the 2 tablespoons reserved mushy strawberry liquid. Drizzle over the almost-cooled cake.

PREACHER'S CHOCOLATE CAKE

My husband and I see eye to eye on most things except how to load a dishwasher . . . and chocolate cake. He always chooses chocolate cake, and I've frankly never tasted a chocolate cake that I couldn't live without. But because chocolate cake is *his* favorite and he's *my* favorite, I vowed to work on a recipe that we could both enjoy! The texture of this cake is perfection—dense and moist, but still light. The vanilla bean buttercream is Heaven! (And truth be told, the icing is the reason I could eat the entire cake myself.) He asks for "chocolate cake with white icing" for every occasion now, which is just fine by me, because this recipe has made me a believer.

For the cake

2 cups cake flour

2 cups sugar

¾ cup (heaping) unsweetened cocoa powder

2 teaspoons baking powder

1½ teaspoons baking soda

1 teaspoon salt

1 cup whole milk, at room temperature

½ cup vegetable oil

2 large eggs, at room temperature

2 teaspoons coffee-flavored extract

2 teaspoons vanilla extract

1 cup boiling water

For the frosting

1 cup unsalted butter, at room temperature

5 cups powdered sugar

⅛ teaspoon salt

3 to 4 tablespoons whole milk

2 teaspoons vanilla extract

⅛ teaspoon almond extract (optional, but I sure love it!)

Set the oven to 350°F. Coat two 9-inch cake pans with nonstick baking spray.

In the bowl of a stand mixer fitted with the paddle attachment, combine the cake flour, sugar, cocoa, baking powder, baking soda, and salt; stir together on low speed until combined. Add the milk, oil, eggs, coffee extract, and vanilla extract to the dry ingredients and mix well on medium speed. Reduce the speed to low and slowly and carefully add the boiling water. Drape a dish towel over the bowl or attach a splash guard, then mix on high speed for 1 minute. Remove the bowl from the mixer and stir with a spoon or rubber spatula to incorporate any batter that is unmixed in the bottom of the bowl.

Carefully pour the batter evenly into the two prepared cake pans and bake for 27 to 30 minutes, or until a toothpick inserted in the center comes out clean. Allow the cakes to cool for 10 minutes in the pans before inverting them onto a cooling rack to cool entirely.

While the cakes are cooling, make the frosting. In a stand mixer fitted with the paddle attachment, beat the butter, 1 cup powdered sugar, and the salt until well blended, stopping to scrape down the sides of the bowl. Add the remaining 4 cups powdered sugar, milk, vanilla extract, and almond extract (if using); beat until smooth, adding more milk, a teaspoon at a time, or more powdered sugar to reach the consistency you prefer.

When the cakes are completely cool, spread a thin layer of frosting on the top of one cake round, spreading all the way to the edges. Set the second cake round on top, then frost the top and sides. Refrigerate the cake to set the frosting. Serve cold, to allow for easier cutting and better flavor.

Note

I heat my water to boiling in the microwave in a glass measuring cup with a spout so I can pour it smoothly and easily.

COMPANY POUND CAKE

I once heard a gal from the way-deep South say that her mama referred to pound cake as "counter cake" because there was always one sitting on the counter. And that is about as accurate a name for anything as I've ever heard. Pound cake has become a kitchen classic because it's made with staple ingredients, it's a cinch to mix up, and it keeps for days, often getting better after it sits. And it can even freeze, so it's at the ready when you need to serve company a little bite of sweet. I have one of these cakes sitting on the counter just about any time we have a round of company. And it has become quite legendary. Just ask around a little . . . or make one for yourself! You'll see why.

FOR THE CAKE

16 tablespoons (2 sticks) unsalted butter, at room temperature
3 cups sugar
6 large eggs, at room temperature
1 cup whole sour cream
3 cups cake flour
½ teaspoon salt
¼ teaspoon baking soda
½ teaspoon rum extract
½ teaspoon coconut extract
½ teaspoon vanilla extract
½ teaspoon butter extract

FOR THE GLAZE

1 cup sugar
½ cup water
1 teaspoon rum extract
1 teaspoon coconut extract
1 teaspoon vanilla extract
1 teaspoon almond extract

Set the oven to 350°F. Coat a large tube pan with nonstick baking spray.

In the bowl of a stand mixer fitted with the paddle attachment, cream the butter and sugar together until light and fluffy. Add the eggs, one at a time, incorporating well after each addition and scraping down the sides of the bowl when necessary. Stir in the sour cream. In a medium bowl, preferably with a pour spout, combine the flour, salt, and baking soda. Slowly beat the flour mixture into the wet ingredients, a third at a time. Then finally beat in the four extracts.

Using a bowl scraper, scrape the bowl and fold in any unmixed ingredients around the sides and in the bottom of the bowl. Pour the batter into the prepared tube pan; spread it around evenly in the pan without pressing down. Bake for 60 to 65 minutes, or until a toothpick inserted in the center comes out clean. Allow to cool in the pan for 10 minutes before turning out onto a cake plate.

While the cake is cooling in the pan, make the glaze. In a small saucepan, combine the sugar, water, and four extracts. Stir over medium heat until the sugar dissolves. After turning the cake out onto a cake plate, slowly, slowly ladle the sugary liquid over the cake, letting it soak in entirely. Allow the cake to cool for another 30 minutes or so before serving.

Note

Because this cake is so fluffy and dreamy, I use my Nordic Ware 18-cup angel food/pound cake pan. It's the absolute perfect pan for this cake!

I always set my timer for 60 minutes when I make this cake because I fear overcooking it! Then I check it in 5-minute intervals to remove it from the oven when it's perfect! Once you lick the beater, you'll understand why it would be a heartbreaker to lose this cake.

SOUR CREAM BLUEBERRY STREUSEL MUFFINS

We host weekend company quite a bit, especially during the fall, because the world orbits around football season for those of us who live in the South. For all the company-having weekends, I like to offer a bite of breakfast that's yummy and beautiful—and can be made ahead. These muffins are perfectly tender, with a crumble topping that gives a light cinnamon-y crunch. It's not unusual to find someone unwrapping one over the sink at 11 pm to satisfy a late-night sweet tooth. But be prepared for your company to invite themselves again. They're that good.

FOR THE TOPPING

4 tablespoons (½ stick) unsalted butter, cubed and at room temperature
½ cup sugar
⅓ cup all-purpose flour
1½ teaspoons ground cinnamon
⅛ teaspoon salt

FOR THE MUFFINS

1½ cups all-purpose flour
¾ cup sugar
2 teaspoons baking powder
½ teaspoon salt
⅓ cup vegetable oil
⅓ cup whole milk
1 large egg, lightly beaten, at room temperature
1 teaspoon vanilla extract
⅓ cup whole sour cream
1 cup blueberries
Salted butter, for serving

Set the oven to 400°F. Coat a 12-cup muffin tin with nonstick baking spray or line it with baking papers.

To make the streusel topping, mix all the ingredients, mashing and incorporating everything with a fork or pastry cutter; set aside.

For the muffins, whisk together the flour, sugar, baking powder, and salt in a large bowl. Make a well in the middle of the dry ingredients and stir in the oil, milk, and egg. Add the vanilla and sour cream and stir well with a wooden spoon. Gently fold in the blueberries without busting them.

Using an ice cream scoop with a release lever, fill the prepared muffin cups just below the top, and heap on the crumb topping mixture.

Bake for 20 minutes, or until a toothpick inserted into the center comes out clean. The muffins should be golden. Don't overbake them.

Cool completely in the muffin tin or else your tops will separate from your bottoms. Gently run a knife around the edges and carefully lift each muffin out of the tin. Replace any crumbly streusel topping that falls off. (Or eat it.) Serve with butter, naturally! Store any leftovers in an airtight container.

HELLO DOLLY BROWNIES

Coconut is at the tippy-top of my Favorite Flavors list. (Well, it's a photo finish between coconut and lemon.) Chocolate, I'm sorry to say, is waaay down on the list for me. However, piling sweet coconut on top of a chocolaty brownie may be the best thing I've ever done. My sister-in-law Nancy always brings Hello Dolly Bars to our gatherings, and I love them like crazy. One night when we were hosting college students here for a movie night, I had an idea to stack an entire pan of Hello Dolly Bars on top of an entire pan of brownies. They were a sweet hit and became a new favorite!

1 family-size box brownie mix
3 large eggs, lightly beaten, at room temperature
½ cup vegetable oil
¼ cup water
1 teaspoon vanilla extract
1 cup graham cracker crumbs
¾ cup milk chocolate chips
¾ cup semisweet chocolate chips
1 cup coconut flakes
¼ cup pecan chips
1 (14-ounce) can sweetened condensed milk
Flaky sea salt

Set the oven to 350°F. Line a 9 x 13-inch baking pan with overlapping sheets of parchment paper, making sure the parchment overhangs the edges of the pan so the brownies can be lifted out easily. Spray the parchment lightly with nonstick baking spray.

In a large bowl, combine the brownie mix, eggs, oil, water, and vanilla. Stir together with a big spoon until combined but not completely smooth. Spread into the prepared pan. Bake for 15 minutes. Gently scatter the graham cracker crumbs over the top of the hot brownies, then the chocolate chips, then the coconut flakes, then the pecan chips. Pour the sweetened condensed milk over the entire pan and top with a few pinches of flaky sea salt. Return to the oven to bake for 25 to 28 minutes, or until the corners are caramelized, the center is set, and the top no longer looks wet. Allow to cool for 20 minutes on the counter, then chill in the refrigerator for at least an hour.

Remove the entire pan of chilled brownies by pulling up on the edges of the parchment. Then cut into 24 squares using a clean, sharp, wet knife.

BLACK AND BLUE BREAD
WITH LEMON GLAZE

Several years ago during the holiday season, I was baking and preparing to have a house full of company. I had multiple open texts and calls going with friends who were also in their kitchens cooking and baking and readying for family and friends. My friend Celeste texted me that she was making a blueberry bread recipe that was one of their family's favorites, and she sent the recipe to me. Over the years, I've made it my own—sweet, tart, and lemony. The texture of this quick bread is like no other, and it makes the most beautiful slices with blackberries and blueberries all throughout! I never make this recipe that I don't double it!

FOR THE BREAD

1½ cups all-purpose flour

1 teaspoon baking powder

1 teaspoon salt

⅛ teaspoon ground cinnamon

½ cup blueberries

½ cup blackberries

1 cup sugar

½ cup whole milk

⅓ cup unsalted butter, melted

2 large eggs, at room temperature

Grated zest of 1 lemon

2 tablespoons freshly squeezed
   lemon juice

FOR THE GLAZE

½ cup powdered sugar

2 tablespoons whole milk

1 tablespoon melted unsalted butter

Grated zest of 1 lemon

Set the oven to 350°F. Coat an 8½ x 4½-inch glass or ceramic loaf pan with nonstick baking spray.

In a medium bowl, stir together the flour, baking powder, salt, and cinnamon. Stir in the blueberries and blackberries, gently tossing to coat them in flour. In another bowl, whisk together the sugar, milk, melted butter, eggs, lemon zest, and lemon juice. Stir the liquid mixture into the flour-berry mixture just until blended. Pour the batter into the prepared pan. Bake for about 1 hour, or until a toothpick inserted in the center comes out clean. Cool in the pan for 10 minutes before turning out onto a cooling rack to cool completely.

While the cake is cooling, make the glaze. Whisk together the powdered sugar, milk, melted butter, and lemon zest. Drizzle over the cooled loaf.

SHEET PAN BANANA CAKE

I'm willing to bet you may consider looking right past this recipe because "sheet pan banana cake" doesn't sound all that exciting compared to some of the other luxurious dessert recipes in this book. But I assure you, this recipe should be made and hallowed. My friend Erin made this cake one weekend when I stayed with her, and it's divine! And it makes a ton, so it has served me well for Bible study, teacher appreciation meals in the lounge, potlucks, picnics, office parties, and more! And you know what? There's never a crumb left!

FOR THE CAKE

8 tablespoons (1 stick) unsalted butter, at room temperature

1½ cups sugar

2 large eggs, at room temperature

1 cup whole sour cream

1 teaspoon vanilla extract

2 cups all-purpose flour

1 teaspoon baking soda

¼ teaspoon salt

2 medium ripe bananas, mashed

FOR THE FROSTING

1 (8-ounce) package cream cheese, at room temperature

8 tablespoons (1 stick) unsalted butter, at room temperature

2 teaspoons vanilla extract

3 to 4 cups powdered sugar

Set the oven to 350°F. Coat a 15 x 10-inch jelly roll pan with nonstick baking spray.

In the bowl of a stand mixer fitted with the paddle attachment, cream the butter and sugar until light and fluffy. Add the eggs, one at a time, mixing until combined. Stir in the sour cream and vanilla. In a separate bowl, combine the flour, baking soda, and salt. Gradually add the dry ingredients to the creamed mixture. Using a spoon, stir in the bananas.

Spread the batter in the prepared pan. Bake for 20 to 25 minutes, or until a toothpick inserted in the center comes out clean. Let cool completely in the pan.

When the cake is cool, make the frosting. In the bowl of a stand mixer fitted with the paddle attachment, beat the cream cheese and butter. Add the vanilla and the powdered sugar, 1 cup at a time, until it's spreading consistency. Spread over the cooled cake.

LEMON RICOTTA PANCAKES

One of my most memorable meals in New York City was at Sarabeth's in TriBeCa several years ago. A girls' trip of 10 moms and daughters all gathered around a long table for brunch. Everyone chose different items from the menu to make certain we could all sample a little something of everything. We shared bites, we swapped entire plates, and we made a great memory. The food was fabulous, and the company was even better. I ordered lemon ricotta pancakes that day; they were the stuff of dreams. I thought about them long after, and as with many restaurant dishes, decided to make them for us at home. Fluffy, tender, creamy, and just faintly lemony. Swoon.

1 cup whole ricotta
⅔ cup whole milk
2 large eggs
3 tablespoons sugar
Grated zest and juice of 1 large
    lemon
1 teaspoon vanilla extract
½ teaspoon grated nutmeg
1 cup all-purpose flour
1 tablespoon baking powder
Salt
Unsalted butter, for the pan
Warmed syrup, for serving
Fresh berries, for serving
Powdered sugar, for serving

In a medium bowl, whisk together the ricotta, milk, eggs, sugar, lemon zest, lemon juice, vanilla, and nutmeg. In a small bowl, whisk together the flour, baking powder, and a pinch of salt. Add the dry ingredients to the wet ingredients and stir gently until just combined; be careful not to overmix. It's okay for the batter to be a little clumpy, which creates good texture. Refrigerate the batter for about a half hour.

Set the oven to 200°F.

Preheat a good nonstick skillet over medium heat. Melt enough butter to cover the bottom of the skillet. Spoon ¼ cup of the batter into the skillet for each pancake; you may be able to fit a few at a time depending on the size of your skillet, but don't let them touch. Allow to cook undisturbed until tiny bubbles form and pop around the very edges. Gently flip, and cook for another few minutes undisturbed, until the sides look tender but cooked. As the pancakes are done, transfer them to a wire rack set over a sheet pan and keep them warm in the oven while you make the remaining pancakes. Serve with warm syrup, fresh berries, and a sprinkling of powdered sugar.

Note

A new favorite update to this recipe that has me over the moon is spreading a layer of tart cherry preserves between your pancakes. Or make my Sour Cherry Compote (page 177) and spoon it over a stack!

EUNA MAE'S LEMON-GLAZED CAKE

My grannie Euna Mae made this cake for every occasion, every birthday, every holiday, and every food-taking party, event, or meeting. It became her signature cake. And I'm telling you what, it is good. It's simple, but it's delicious and has made generations of folks very happy. She swore by sifting the powdered sugar in the glaze, which is a step I don't always take. But sometimes for the sake of nostalgia (and just in case she's watching from Heaven), I sift and think about her.

FOR THE CAKE

1 box lemon supreme cake mix
3 tablespoons all-purpose flour
1 (3.4-ounce) package lemon instant pudding
¾ cup vegetable oil
¾ cup water
½ cup freshly squeezed lemon juice
1 teaspoon vanilla extract
4 large eggs, at room temperature

FOR THE GLAZE

2 to 3 cups sifted powdered sugar
2 to 4 tablespoons freshly squeezed lemon juice
1 teaspoon vanilla extract

Set the oven to 350°F. Coat a Bundt pan with nonstick baking spray.

In the bowl of a stand mixer fitted with the paddle attachment, combine the cake mix, flour, pudding mix, oil, water, lemon juice, and vanilla on medium speed. Add the eggs, one at a time, then beat on medium for 2 minutes. Pour the batter into the prepared Bundt pan.

Bake for 40 minutes, or until a toothpick inserted in the middle comes out clean. Allow to cool for 10 minutes before inverting onto a cake plate, then cool completely.

While the cake is cooling, make the glaze. Whisk together 2 cups powdered sugar, 2 tablespoons lemon juice, and the vanilla until smooth, adding up to 1 cup more powdered sugar to thicken it or up to 2 tablespoons more lemon juice to thin it, until it's the perfect consistency. When you hold up a spoon and let the glaze fall off the end of it, it should fall smoothly but slowly like honey. Drizzle the glaze over the cooled cake.

DOUBLE CHOCOLATE BLONDIES

A blondie is more or less a cousin to the brownie, having no cocoa powder in the dough but being loaded with chocolate chips instead. I'm not even a chocolate girl, and I love these! Pay close attention to the baking time, and don't leave them one more minute in the oven than the recipe calls for. Serve them completely cooled, or scoop them when they're still warm and gooey into bowls and top with good vanilla ice cream. Either way, these buttery, rich blondies are a crowd-pleaser!

2 cups all-purpose flour
1 teaspoon baking soda
1 teaspoon salt
½ teaspoon ground cinnamon
16 tablespoons (2 sticks) unsalted butter, at room temperature
1 cup light brown sugar
½ cup white sugar
2 teaspoons vanilla extract
2 large eggs, at room temperature
1 cup semisweet chocolate chips
1 cup milk chocolate chips

Set the oven to 350°F. Coat a 9 x 13-inch baking pan with nonstick baking spray.

In a medium bowl, preferably with a pour spout, whisk together the flour, baking soda, salt, and cinnamon. Set aside.

In the bowl of a stand mixer fitted with the paddle attachment, mix the butter, brown sugar, and white sugar on low speed to incorporate, then cream on high speed for a few minutes, scraping down the sides of the bowl as needed. It should be light and fluffy. Reduce the speed to low, add the vanilla, and then add the eggs, one at a time, mixing until combined. With the mixer still on low, add the flour mixture a little at a time. Mix until incorporated. You'll have more of a dough than a batter. Using a heavy wooden spoon, stir in the chips by hand.

Spread the dough in the prepared pan and bake for 29 minutes. No more, no less. Remove the pan from the oven and allow to cool for 10 minutes before cutting into squares if you want them gooey. Or let them cool entirely if you want cleaner cut bars.

LOVERLY LEMON BARS

You know the age-old question "If you had only one food to eat for the rest of your life, what would it be?" My answer? Lemon bars. You see, I come from a long line of lemon lovers. And these lemon bars scratch every lemon itch I've ever had. They are tart and sweet, with a mouthwatering shortbread crust underneath. For the love of Pete, please use real lemon juice and real lemon zest. You'll not be disappointed!

FOR THE CRUST
16 tablespoons (2 sticks) unsalted butter, at room temperature
½ cup powdered sugar, plus more for sprinkling
Salt
Grated zest of 1 lemon
2 cups all-purpose flour

FOR THE CUSTARD
4 large eggs plus 1 additional yolk
1½ cups sugar
Grated zest of 4 lemons
¾ cup freshly squeezed lemon juice

Set the oven to 350°F. Coat a 9 x 13-inch baking pan with nonstick baking spray.

In the bowl of a stand mixer fitted with the paddle attachment, cream the butter and powdered sugar. Add a pinch of salt, the lemon zest, and the flour, 1 cup at a time. Mix just until combined and still a bit craggy. Pour the crumbly dough into the prepared pan. Use your hands to break up the dough into loose clumps and arrange the clumps around the pan. Then lay a piece of parchment over the pan and use your hands to press and spread the dough around to fill the pan. Press down well and make it as smooth as possible. Remove the parchment sheet, and refrigerate for 20 minutes.

Bake for 20 minutes, or until golden. Remove from the oven. Turn the oven down to 325°F. In a bowl, whisk together the eggs, sugar, lemon zest, and lemon juice. Carefully pour the lemony liquid over the crust. Bake for an additional 25 to 28 minutes, or until the lemon custard is set. There will be small bubbles in the top. Remove from the oven and allow to cool completely in the pan. Dust the top with sifted powdered sugar. Cut into squares with a wet knife, wiping any custard or crumbs off the knife and moistening it again before each cut.

HOMEMADE DOUBLE-FROSTED CINNAMON ROLLS

I grew up eating cinnamon toast. My mother made it for me and my brother many mornings before school. Thus, my adoration of cinnamon, sugar, and butter blossomed early in my lifetime. My preferred version of this beloved trinity is in the form of a mouthwatering, gooey cinnamon roll. Some recipes call for a glaze, while other recipes call for cream cheese frosting. But because of my undying devotion to gooey, messy, buttery, sugary cinnamon rolls, my recipe is both glazed and frosted. Y'all, they're so good you just won't believe. This recipe may seem long, but it's because I'm telling you everything you need to know so you're set up for success! The finished pans of rolls will make your heart sing! Worth. Every. Step.

FOR THE DOUGH
1½ cups whole milk
8 tablespoons (1 stick) unsalted butter, cut into pieces
½ cup + 1 teaspoon sugar
½ cup very warm water
1 package active dry yeast
3 large eggs, lightly beaten
2 teaspoons salt
6 cups all-purpose flour, plus more for kneading and rolling

Set the oven to 200°F to create a warm place for the first rise.

For the dough, pour the milk into a small saucepan and bring to a simmer over medium-low heat. Remove the pan from the heat and stir in the butter and ½ cup sugar; let cool.

Meanwhile, in a small bowl, gently whisk together the warm water, yeast, and remaining 1 teaspoon sugar until dissolved. Allow to rest for 10 minutes until it's foamy.

In the bowl of a stand mixer fitted with the dough hook, combine the cooled milk mixture, yeast mixture, eggs, salt, and 3 cups of the flour and mix on low speed until smooth. Add the remaining 3 cups flour, ½ cup at a time, and mix until a smooth ball forms. Scrape out the dough onto a generously floured work surface. It will be very sticky. Shake a little extra flour over the dough and knead for about 5 minutes, until the dough is combined and smooth and a gentle finger-poke in the top presses in but slowly springs back a little.

Now turn off the oven.

Place the dough in a large greased bowl, cover with a lightweight dish towel that is barely damp, and let it rise in the warmed oven until it has doubled in bulk, 60 to 70 minutes. It will spread and fill the bowl more than it will actually rise up. After 30 to 35 minutes, you may turn the oven back on to 200°F for just a minute and

For the filling

1½ cups sugar, plus more
for sprinkling in the pan
16 tablespoons (2 sticks)
unsalted butter, at room
temperature
so it's spreadable
¼ cup ground cinnamon

For the glaze

3 cups powdered sugar
5 tablespoons unsalted butter,
melted
7 tablespoons whole milk,
at room temperature
1 teaspoon vanilla extract
¼ teaspoon almond extract

(ingredients continue)

then turn it off quickly to maintain a little heat in there. After the dough has doubled, remove the bowl from the oven.

Set the oven to 200°F again to create a warm place for the second rise. Coat two 9 x 13-inch baking pans with nonstick baking spray, then sprinkle the bottom of the pans with a little sugar. Yum, right?!

Turn out the dough onto a floured surface and punch the dough a few times with a firm fist to let the air out. Sprinkle with a little flour as needed to keep it from being too sticky. Roll the dough into a rectangle approximately 12 x 36 inches. (You may wish to cut the dough in half and work in two batches for the sake of space.) Spread the dough with the very soft butter and cover generously with the sugar and cinnamon. Starting with one long end, roll the dough into a tight log and pinch the edges together to seal. Cut the log into 1½-inch-thick slices. Lay the cinnamon roll slices in the pans so they're just touching.

Now turn off the oven.

Cover the rolls with a lightweight dish towel and place the pans in the oven for a second rise. Allow to rise for at least 40 minutes, or until the rolls have doubled in size and are squished up next to each other. Remove the pans from the oven and set the oven to 350°F.

Remove the towel and bake the rolls for about 25 minutes, until golden brown but not terribly brown or they'll be dry. Begin checking the rolls at 20 minutes and then check again every 2 or 3 minutes until done.

While the cinnamon rolls are baking, make the glaze. Stir together the powdered sugar, melted butter, milk, and extracts until smooth. The glaze should be thin enough that it will ooze down into the crevices of the cinnamon rolls.

(recipe continues)

FOR THE CREAM CHEESE FROSTING

1 (8-ounce) package cream cheese, at room temperature
3 tablespoons unsalted butter, at room temperature
1 teaspoon vanilla extract
¼ teaspoon almond extract
Salt
¼ cup whole milk
3 cups powdered sugar

Next, make the cream cheese frosting. In the bowl of a stand mixer fitted with the paddle attachment, beat the cream cheese and butter until light, scraping down the sides of the bowl. Beat in the extracts and a pinch of salt. Then add the milk and 2 cups of the powdered sugar; beat until smooth. Add the remaining 1 cup powdered sugar and beat until smooth. Scrape down the sides of bowl and use a whisk to mix in any ingredients that haven't combined.

When the rolls are finished, allow them to rest for 2 or 3 minutes. Drizzle each cinnamon roll with 1 to 2 tablespoons of glaze, making sure to get it into the grooves. Then slather the tops with cream cheese frosting. Pour some milk and serve!

Note

Resist the urge to open and close the door while the dough is rising. If you must near the end of each rising period, open and close the door quickly and gently.

To make these ahead, prepare them all the way up to the baking step. At that point, parbake them for about 12 minutes in small aluminum foil pans. Remove the pans from the oven and allow the rolls to cool completely. Cover the pans tightly with plastic wrap, then aluminum foil, and slide each one into a gallon-size zip-top bag. Seal and store in the freezer for up to 6 weeks. Let them thaw overnight in the refrigerator before you plan to serve them. Uncover and bake at 350°F for 10 to 12 minutes, or until they're nicely golden brown. Glaze and frost them per the recipe.

SIMPLE SALTED
CHOCOLATE CHIP COOKIES

I looked for what seemed like my whole life for *the* chocolate chip cookie recipe of my dreams. I wanted them to be chewy but crisp. Cakey but still gooey. And I finally landed on this recipe. I have made these cookies for more people than I can count because chocolate chip cookies are always a good idea. Many years ago I shared a similar recipe on my food blog, but it had entirely too many things to measure and more effort than chocolate chip cookies should require. So I've given that recipe a make-under—but with a few new steps that truly send them over the moon!

3⅔ cups all-purpose flour

1½ teaspoons salt

1½ teaspoons baking powder

1¼ teaspoons baking soda

1¼ teaspoons ground cinnamon

2½ sticks unsalted butter, at room temperature

1¼ cups light brown sugar

1 cup plus 2 tablespoons white sugar

2 large eggs, at room temperature

2 teaspoons vanilla extract

1½ cups semisweet chocolate chips

1½ cups milk chocolate chips

Sea salt, for sprinkling

Set the oven to 350°F. Line a sheet pan with parchment or a silicone baking mat. Clear a space in the freezer large enough to fit your sheet pan. Lay a wire cooling rack down to protect your freezer shelf.

In a large bowl, whisk together the flour, salt, baking powder, baking soda, and cinnamon. Set aside.

In the bowl of a stand mixer fitted with the paddle attachment, cream the butter and sugars together until very light, about 5 minutes on medium speed. Scrape down the sides of the bowl as needed. Add the eggs, one at a time, mixing well after each addition. On low speed, add the vanilla. Continuing on low, add the dry ingredients in two additions, mixing just until combined. Do not overmix the dough! Using a heavy wooden spoon, stir in the chocolate chips.

Using a rounded 3½-ounce ice cream scoop or ⅓-cup measure, scoop 6 mounds of dough onto the prepared sheet pan, using your hands to make them rounded and smooth. They will be the size of generous golf balls. Sprinkle each dough ball with a bit of sea salt and bake for 12 minutes. Remove from the oven, drop the sheet pan flat on the counter so the cookies settle, then place the entire sheet pan in the freezer for 10 minutes. Remove the sheet pan from the freezer and use a spatula to transfer the cookies to a cooling rack to rest. Repeat with the remaining dough.

EUNA MAE'S "PEACH" FRIED PIES

Here they are: Euna Mae's fried pies. She was known for them. It was a labor of love for her to make these for us, and everyone knew it and was grateful. She passed down this recipe to me over the years, little bit by little bit, one conversation at a time. She'd tell me tidbits like using refrigerated pie dough because it was hardier than homemade and how it was imperative to fry the pies in Crisco shortening rather than oil. She even giggled to me one time about how everyone referred to them as peach fried pies, even though she used dried apricots because she liked their texture better. Every smell and each bite makes us think of her still.

13 to 14 ounces dried apricots, quartered

¾ cup sugar

¼ teaspoon ground cinnamon

½ teaspoon vanilla extract

Grated zest of 1 lemon

3 refrigerated pie dough rounds

1 large egg white

2 cups Crisco shortening

In a small saucepan, combine the quartered apricots, sugar, and cinnamon. Add just enough water to come right to the top of the fruit and stir. Bring the water to a boil over medium heat, stirring to dissolve the sugar. Cover, turn the heat down to low, and simmer, stirring occasionally, for an hour or so, or until the fruit is tender and starting to come apart. Be careful not to let the fruit get brown or tough. Remove the pan from the heat and use two forks to pull and shred the apricots in the pan. Stir in the vanilla and lemon zest. Cover and set aside.

Allow the sleeves of pie dough to sit at room temperature for about 10 minutes before unrolling them. Working on a silicone baking mat or parchment paper, use a 5-inch bowl and a paring knife to trace circles in one pie dough round. You should be able to fit 3 circles. Then roll out the dough scraps, making enough to cut one more 5-inch circle. Discard any remaining scraps. Repeat with the remaining two pie dough rounds. You should get 12 circles in total.

In a small bowl, use a fork to whisk the egg white with a splash of water until the white loosens up a little. Scoop about 2 tablespoons of fruit filling into the center of each pie dough round. Dip your fingers in the egg wash and wipe it around the rim of each pie dough round. Fold over to make a half moon, pressing the seams together. Crimp or use the tines of a fork to secure the seam. Use your fingers to gently press down the belly of the pies where the filling is so that they're as uniform in shape as possible, with no bulging. Transfer to a sheet pan lined with parchment and refrigerate for 10 minutes.

Meanwhile, melt the shortening in a large cast iron skillet over medium heat. The oil is ready when it begins to shimmer. Fry the pies in batches, 1½ to 2 minutes per side, until they're golden brown and crisp. Transfer to a paper towel–lined plate or brown paper grocery bags to drain and cool. Store in a brown paper bag with the top folded over and clipped closed.

Note

You may wish to dust the pies with sifted powdered sugar. We always had them plain, but powdered sugar is never a bad idea.

CHOCOLATE PEANUT BUTTER DREAM PIE

This is easily the sweetest, richest dessert in this book. Actually, it's the sweetest, richest, dessert that I make, period. I once made two of these pies for a group of my son Luke's high school friends, thinking for sure they'd eat them both. But they could hardly finish their little slices! They never even touched the second pie! It's creamy and thick, peanut buttery and chocolaty. And then it's topped with chopped peanut butter cups and a chocolate drizzle. Listen up: You will need cold milk at the ready!

2 cups chocolate cookie crumbs

8 tablespoons (1 stick) unsalted butter, melted

¾ cup creamy peanut butter

4 ounces (half of an 8-ounce package) cream cheese, at room temperature

1½ cup powdered sugar

½ teaspoon vanilla extract

1 (8-ounce) carton Cool Whip, thawed

1 to 2 cups chopped chocolate peanut butter cups

¼ cup semisweet chocolate chips

¼ cup milk chocolate chips

2 tablespoons coconut oil

In a small bowl, combine the cookie crumbs and melted butter with a fork until the crumbs are moist. Pour the crumbs into a 9-inch pie plate and press into the bottom and up the sides. Refrigerate the crumb crust while you prepare the filling so it firms up a little.

In the bowl of a stand mixer fitted with the paddle attachment, beat the peanut butter and cream cheese with the powdered sugar and vanilla. On low speed, stir in the thawed Cool Whip. Carefully spread the peanut butter filling into the chilled crumb crust. Cover the top with the chopped peanut butter cups.

In a small microwaveable bowl or glass measuring cup, melt the chocolate chips and coconut oil for 20 seconds at a time until smooth, stirring between each interval. Using a small spoon, drizzle the melted chocolate all over the top of the pie. Chill for at least 1 hour before serving.

FANCY CINNAMON TOAST
WITH STRAWBERRIES,
HONEY, AND GOAT CHEESE

Some nights I get such a strong sweet tooth that I've been known to start making a pie from scratch at 10 pm, which is absurd! So in order to satisfy my late-night cravings, I've concocted this quick, satisfying treat that is easy to make and a healthier option than pie. (Although pie is my favorite, let's be clear.) Crispy, buttery cinnamon toast loaded with fresh strawberries and a drizzle of honey gets a touch of "grown up" with the addition of crumbled goat cheese. This number does the trick when I just need a little bite of sweet.

1 slice good farmhouse
  white bread
Salted butter, at room
  temperature
1 tablespoon cinnamon-sugar
2 or 3 strawberries, thinly
  sliced
Honey
Crumbled goat cheese
  (optional)

Preheat the broiler.

Toast the bread in a toaster on a very low setting to get a light golden color. Transfer to a sheet pan, butter the bread generously, and sprinkle the top with cinnamon-sugar. Place under the broiler for a minute or two, with the door cracked open, until it's brown and bubbly on top. Remove from the broiler, top with layers of sliced strawberries, a good drizzle of honey, and a little crumbled goat cheese if you'd like.

RECIPES THAT
GATHER AND GIVE

The people who give you their food give you their heart.
—Cesar Chavez

Recipes THAT Gather

OVER THE YEARS of inviting folks into my home to share food, I've developed a few menus that I go to time and time again. Having a meal or two built with the purpose of gathering people helps increase my willingness to be hospitable because it takes out the guesswork! Sam and I could practically make these meals in our sleep! Many of the recipes in these menus can be made ahead so your time in the kitchen is manageable. Crowd-pleasing, delicious, and tried-and-true, these menus are for casual, everyday get-togethers—our favorite kind! I've teed it up for you to fill bellies so that you can open your homes and fill hearts. Let it be said that I always overestimate food quantities because it would grieve my soul to run out. So when in doubt, I fix boatloads of food and send home all the leftovers in little take-out containers with handwritten reheating instructions. That way the food keeps on giving long after the gathering has ended.

ENCHILADAS

Who doesn't love Mexican food?! The enchiladas can be filled, covered, and stored in the fridge until time to bake. The beans, salsa, and sweets can be made ahead of time too! Put out your biggest bowl of tortilla chips!

Cream Cheese Chicken Enchiladas, 108

Baked Jalapeño Refried Beans, 136

Everyday Salsa, 174

Loaded Southern Guacamole, 28

Preacher's Chocolate Cake, 186

BARBECUE

This is our number one meal -that we fix for large groups or multiple families. The meat, beans, slaw, chow-chow, and cake can be prepared ahead of time. And I serve it with buttered, toasted Texas toast!

Sam's Smoked Pulled Pork, 63
or
Braised Pulled Pork, 68

Euna Mae's Macaroni and Cheese, 140

Spicy Skillet BBQ Beans, 131

Anytime Slaw, 38

Pickled Chow-Chow, page 50

Gran's Strawberry Cake, 184

Simple Salted Chocolate Chip Cookies, 211

CHILI & GRITS

This comfort meal is the one I serve when I have more people than I have chairs! Just put out sturdy bowls and have guests load up on chili, grits, and crackers! It's casual, it's filling, and it can be prepared in advance!

Brown Sugar Chili over Cheese Grits, 90

Texas Firecrackers, 8

Homemade Double-Frosted Cinnamon Rolls, 206

Recipes THAT *Give*

IN MY EARLY TWENTIES, shortly after I was married, a gal named Betty Gaddy left a magnificent imprint on me. She modeled for me how to tune my heart to hear the needs of others and then to respond. She showed up at my door one afternoon with cough medicine and comfort food after hearing that I was home sick with young babies who were also ill. There is something special about being on the receiving end of good, thoughtful food when we have need, isn't there? We've all had something in our lives that has turned us upside down for a day or two, a few weeks, or an entire season. Sickness, sadness, loss, change, tragedy. And sometimes we're just simply overwhelmed. I've walked those roads and been loved on by people who served me and my family with food, some homemade and some take-out. It loved our hearts. We felt cared for. Shared food also can be given to welcome and greet, to say hello and thank-you, and to communicate that someone is on your heart. Here are several menus that I have compiled that are easy to make and give. They travel, they reheat, they comfort, and they warm hearts. Food that gives doesn't have to be complicated, it only has to be shared.

FULL MEALS

Comfort Chicken Pot Pie, 101
Euna Mae's Lemon-Glazed Cake, 200

Hearty Homemade Chicken and
Dumplins, 92
Mama's Cranberry Salad, 41
Chocolate Peanut Butter Dream Pie, 215

Creamy Pesto Tortellini Soup, 95
Store-bought salad and bread
Hello Dolly Brownies, 195

Cream Cheese Chicken Enchiladas, 108
Everyday Salsa, 174
Simple Salted Chocolate Chip
Cookies, 211

FUN TREATS

Sour Cream Blueberry Streusel
Muffins, 193

Everyday Salsa, 174

Easy Refrigerator Pickles, 32

Loverly Lemon Bars, 204

Company Pound Cake, 189

GRATITUDE

I get entirely overwhelmed when I think about how grateful I am for this opportunity to write a book that shares my heart. And I become equally weepy when I think about the people in my world who have stood on the hill and prayed for me and cheered me on.

To Sam Hannon: What have I done to deserve you? You are my biggest cheerleader and the best thing that has ever happened to my heart next to Jesus. You make me believe I can do anything. Thank you for making me laugh, for supporting this hospitality journey from kitchen store to cooking show to cookbook, and for your encouragement and patience. I'd never want anyone else to be my Chief Recipe Tester. Let's grow old eating shrimp and grits together.

To my kids: Oh my word. Grace, Luke, and Isaac, you three are my heart and my purpose. I have wanted nothing more than to make a home for you and Daddy that felt warm, safe, and full of joy. A place where you and your friends felt welcomed. A place where your favorite memories would be made. I hope when you think of me and of home that you think of Jesus, good food, hugs, laughs, and cake.

To Beth: How in the world would this book or this dream have happened without your brains, your creativity, your humor, and your hands? I am beyond grateful for your contribution, but more so for your friendship. Thanks for being loyal and so much fun. Good grief, we do have fun.

To my shop girls who manned the ship so beautifully while I was working on this book: You gals are the best! Your smiles, your warm welcomes, and your hospitality are so much of what brings people back to Euna Mae's time and time again.

To Rachel, Robyn, Allison, Selena, and Jenessa: Thank you for sharing your kitchens with me and for offering your help! You lightened my load and blessed my heart!

To my agent, Shannon Marven (Dupree Miller): Thank you for recognizing my heart, for valuing my message, for trusting my recipes, and for pursuing me with diligence and passion. You have no idea how humbled I am that you believe in me and have worked so hard on my behalf.

To Rolf Zettersten and Patsy Jones: Thank you for your faith in a first-time cookbook author, and special thanks to Keren Baltzer for your expertise and commitment to making this cookbook a beautiful experience for everyone who reads it.

To the people of Fellowship Bible Church NWA: Thank you for allowing me decades of opportunities to share my heart and home. You have modeled hospitality and kindness to my family more times than I can count. Your fingerprints are everywhere.

To the Euna Mae's community: You have no idea how you have blessed me. I am filled up by your faithfulness and humbled by your patronage. Thank you for believing in the Love Welcome Serve message and for living it out in your own hearts and homes. Here's to intentional kitchening together!

And finally to the Lord Jesus who gave me joy and purpose that I cannot keep to myself: Thank you for making all the difference in my life. May I live a life worthy.

Recipe Index

Recipe Index

Recipe Index

Recipe Index

INDEX